ANTIGUA, BARBUDA, ST. KITTS & NEVIS

ALIVE!

Paris Permenter & John Bigley

HUNTER

HUNTER PUBLISHING, INC,
130 Campus Drive, Edison, NJ 08818
732-225-1900; 800-255-0343; fax 732-417-1744
hunterp@bellsouth.net

Ulysses Travel Publications
4176 Saint-Denis, Montréal, Québec
Canada H2W 2M5
514-843-9882, ext. 2232; fax 514-843-9448

Windsor Books
The Boundary, Wheatley Road, Garsington
Oxford, OX44 9EJ England
01865-361122; fax 01865-361133

ISBN 1-55650-880-8

Maps by Kim André, © 2001 Hunter Publishing, Inc.

1   2   3   4

About The Authors

John Bigley and Paris Permenter fell in love with the Caribbean over a dozen years ago and have turned their extensive knowledge of the region into an occupation. As professional travel writers and photographers, the pair contributes travel articles and photographs on the US and the Caribbean to many national consumer and trade publications. The husband-and-wife team has also written several guidebooks.

Paris and John are the authors of numerous Hunter guides: *Adventure Guide to the Cayman Islands*; *Adventure Guide to Anguilla, Antigua, St. Barts, St. Kitts & St. Martin*; *Cayman Islands Alive!*; *Adventure Guide to Jamaica*; *Jamaica: A Taste of the Island*; *Jamaica Alive!*; *Nassau and the Best of the Bahamas Alive!*; *Romantic Escapes in the Caribbean*; and *Bahamas: A Taste of the Islands*.

Paris and John are also frequent television and radio talk show guests on the subject of travel. Both are members of the Society of American Travel Writers (SATW) and the American Society of Journalists and Authors (ASJA).

Readers can follow the couple's travels on their websites: Travels with Paris and John (www.parisandjohn.com) and Lovetripper Romantic Travel Magazine (www.lovetripper.com).

www.hunterpublishing.com

Hunter's full range of guides to all corners of the globe is featured on our exciting website. You'll find guidebooks to suit every type of traveler, no matter what their budget, lifestyle, or idea of fun.

Adventure Guides – There are now over 30 titles in this series, covering destinations from Alaska's Inside Passage and the Yucatán to Tampa Bay & Florida's West Coast, Montana and Belize. Complete information on what to do, as well as where to stay and eat, *Adventure Guides* are tailor-made for the active traveler, with a focus on hiking, biking, canoeing, horseback riding, trekking, skiing, watersports, and all other kinds of fun.

Alive Guides – This ever-popular line of books takes a unique look at the best each destination offers: fine dining, jazz clubs, first-class class hotels and resorts. In-margin icons direct the reader at a glance. Top-sellers include: *The Cayman Islands, St. Martin & St. Barts,* and *Aruba, Bonaire & Curaçao.*

Our **Rivages Hotels of Character & Charm** books are top sellers, with titles covering France, Spain, Italy, Paris and Portugal. Originating in Paris, they set the standard for excellence with their fabulous color photos, superb maps and candid descriptions of the most remarkable hotels of Europe.

Our **Romantic Weekends** guidebooks provide a series of escapes for couples of all ages and lifestyles. Unlike most "romantic" travel books, ours cover more than charming hotels and delightful restaurants, with a host of activities that you and your partner will remember.

Contents

Maps

Introduction

The Caribbean holds a special place in the hearts of travelers. Some of the region's most special treasures are found in small packages – islands whose petite sizes belie their many activities.

In this region lie two pairs of islands that offer travelers a little of everything in easy-to-reach packages. Whether you want sun-worshipping, or sailing, scuba diving or shopping, you'll find it somewhere among these island twosomes – St. Kitts and Nevis, and Antigua and Barbuda.

Both island sets are part of a chain of islands known as the Leewards, the northern chain of islands that forms demarcation line between the placid Caribbean Sea and the tumultuous Atlantic Ocean.

While both pairs of islands have a British heritage combined with a West Indian atmosphere, they are each unique destinations, charming travelers with their own special assets. The island you select will depend on your interests, the type of accommodation you're seeking, and your plans for activity.

The Attractions

A vacationer in St. Kitts, Nevis, Antigua, or Barbuda is presented with a full menu of activity options. Whatever your choice – golf or gambling, scuba diving or shopping, bird-watching or bicycling – you'll find it on at least one of these islands. The trick is selecting the right island, and that's what this book is all about.

These islands draw many repeat visitors. Their secrets? St. Kitts and Nevis offer visitors these charms:

- a genuine West Indian atmosphere
- a relaxed pace
- beautiful, mountainous terrain
- excellent windsurfing
- superb diving
- the Caribbean's largest number of plantation inns
- fine dining
- numerous unique eco-tourism options

Here are just a few of Antigua's charms:

- great weather
- world-class sailing
- good scuba diving
- duty-free shopping
- easy accessibility

- ◎ luxurious accommodations
- ◎ casino gambling
- ◎ excellent beaches

Tiny Barbuda has other assets:

- ◎ excellent bird-watching
- ◎ good beaches
- ◎ a quiet, secluded atmosphere

Layout

Major Cities

The two major cities in these islands are St. John's in Antigua and Basseterre in St. Kitts. Here you'll find international airports and all the services needed by travelers. Both cities are compact and easy to navigate.

Farther Afield

Most tourism activity is found on St. Kitts and Antigua. Far quieter than many Caribbean islands, these islands offer plenty of quiet getaway options, especially along St. Kitts' Southeast Peninsula.

Beyond these islands, you'll find that Nevis and Barbuda are quieter still. Nevis is little changed from its early tourism days. Barbuda is visited by very few vacationers, although it attracts plenty of birds.

$ The Cost

These islands are not the mass tourism destinations of Nassau, Jamaica, or Aruba, so you'll find that far fewer discount packages are available. Exactly how much you spend will vary not just with your airfare but also with your accommodations. Each of these islands offers accommodations in a full range of prices, with costs varying greatly with the season.

High Season Brings High Prices

Look for higher prices during the winter months. Prices really reach their peak during the Christmas holiday and New Year's. Generally, prices drop in mid-April. During summer months, prices are at their lowest, falling to a real low in August and September, the height of hurricane season. Check with individual properties for exact dates of price breaks.

The Alive! Price Scale

Prices change as quickly as the sand shifts on a beach. For that reason, we've stayed away from providing dollar and cents figures. Besides the constantly changing prices, providers of accommodations offer a wide variety in their price scale as well: partial ocean view, full ocean view, ocean-side, garden view, the list goes on and on. These prices also vary, based on the month and the day of the week, so when you make your reservation, check on all the categories.

For accommodations, our price scale is designed to give you a ballpark figure for a typical stay during peak season. We've based these estimates on high season for a standard room for two persons. These figures don't take into account additional amenities such as meal plans, dive packages, greens fees, etc. Prices are given in US dollars.

We've indicated which island attractions charge admission and which are free.

Alive! Price Scale, Accommodations

For accommodations, our price scale is designed to give you a ballpark figure for a typical stay during peak season. We've based these estimates on high season for a standard room for two persons. These figures don't take into account additional amenities such as meal plans, dive packages, greens fees, etc. Prices are given in US dollars.

At any hotel, be sure to conserve water whenever you can. Fresh water is a precious commodity on most of these islands.

All of our hotel selections take major credit cards, are air conditioned, and have private baths, except in the case of the few guest houses where noted.

All prices are in US dollars.
Deluxe . . . . $301+
Expensive . . . . $201-$300
Moderate . . . . $100-$200
Inexpensive . . . . Under $100

Alive! Price Scale, Dining

For dining, we've set up a price scale based on a three-course dinner that includes appetizer or soup, an entrée, and dessert and coffee. Cocktails and wine are extra.

Prices are per person in US dollars.
Expensive............$40+ per person
Moderate ....$25-$40
Inexpensive ....Under $25

# Planning Your Trip

So where should you go? The decision will depend on many factors:

- ☺ *How long can you stay?* If this is a quick getaway of just three or four nights, select a destination that's easy close to an airport. Antigua is the easiest of the four islands to reach, followed by St. Kitts.

- ☺ *How much seclusion do you want?* If it's peace and quiet you're after, move past the main tourist spots. Nevis and Barbuda are the quietest of the four islands.

- ☺ *What type of accommodations do you want? Are you looking for an all-inclusive, a small inn, or something in-between?* St. Kitts and Nevis have numerous small inns, many housed in historic great houses. Antigua has the largest collection of all-inclusive properties among the four islands, although you'll also find the Jack Tar Resort on St. Kitts. Barbuda is home to one of the most exclusive properties in the Caribbean, the K Club.

☺ *Are you interested in nightlife?* If it's nightlife you're after, set your sights on Antigua, home to both discos and several small casinos. Nightlife is quieter on St. Kitts, which offers a casino and charming island happenings, often to the sound of steel pan bands. Nightlife is very quiet on Nevis and Barbuda.

☺ *Do you want to shop?* Antigua's capital city of St. John's has the best shopping in these islands. Shopping is much more limited in St. Kitts and very hard to find in Nevis and Barbuda.

Types of Accommodations

Whatever you're looking for in the way of accommodations – highrise hotel, seaside bungalow, bed-and-breakfast inn, small traditional hotel – you'll find it on at least one of these islands.

Just as varied as the types of accommodations is the range of prices. Everything from budget motels with Spartan furnishings to private islands that attract royalty and Hollywood types is available. This guidebook covers things in between, places where the everyday vacationers can enjoy safety and comfort. The resorts, hotels, and villas featured on these pages provide for all levels of activity. Some offer around-the-clock fun and evening theme parties for their guests; others point the way for guests to find their own entertainment. Some are full-service properties with everything from beauty salons, jewelry shops, and a half-dozen bars and restaurants located right on the property; others are simple accommodations where the guests have the facilities to cook their own meals.

It is important to choose accommodations carefully. You'll find that an island hotel, unlike a property in a downtown US city, for example, becomes your home away from home. This is not just where you spend your nights, but also a good portion of your days, languishing on the beach, lying beneath towering palms, and luxuriating in a warm sea.

What form will your paradise take? White sandy beaches? Highrise excitement? A resort with daily activities and a pulsating nightlife? A spa where you can select from a menu of luxurious treatments? Or a quiet getaway where the only footprints in the sand are your own?

The choice is yours.

All-Inclusive Resorts

As the name suggests, all-inclusive means that all activities, meals, drinks, airport transfers, and tips are included in the price. Antigua is home to several all-inclusive properties such as Sandals, Sunsail, and others; you'll find Jack Tar on St. Kitts.

This all-inclusive policy means that you're free to try anything you like without worrying about spending your vacation budget for the next five years. Ever been curious about windsurfing? Take a lesson. Want to know how to reggae dance? Throw off your shoes and jump in line. Wonder how those brightly colored drinks with the funny umbrellas taste? Belly up to the bar. You're free to try it all.

Some folks don't like all-inclusive resorts because of the concern (not unfounded) that once you've paid for the whole package you'll be unlikely to leave the property to sample local restaurants and explore the island.

We love all-inclusive resorts, but we are careful to balance a stay there with island tours or visits to off-property restaurants. Even with these extra expenditures, we've found most of these resorts to be economical choices.

Intimate Inns

If you're looking for peace and quiet, small inns offer good getaways and a chance to immerse yourself in more of the local atmosphere. St. Kitts and Nevis are home to the largest concentration of plantation inns in the Caribbean.

It's that opportunity to meet local residents, taste island dishes, and retreat from the typical resort experience that brings travelers to the islands' all-too-often-overlooked small inns.

Just as you would if booking a B&B in the US, ask plenty of questions before booking a stay in a small inn. These properties may offer limited services and may be more restrictive. If applicable, be sure to ask:

- ◎ Are children allowed as guests?
- ◎ Are private tables available or are meals served family style?
- ◎ Are special dietary considerations met?
- ◎ Does a remote location necessitate a rental car?
- ◎ Is breakfast served at one time or as guests wander in?
- ◎ Is smoking permitted indoors?
- ◎ Is there a minimum stay?

Caribbean Dining

For most visitors, dining is an important part of their trip. Dishes are rich with flavor and are often spicy. Some dishes trace their origin back to the earliest days of the island when the Arawak Indians first barbecued meats. Later, distinctive seasonings were developed by Africans who came to the islands as slaves.

Here's a sampling of island dishes found on many local menus:

- ⓢ **Conch** (pronounced konk), a shellfish served chopped, battered, and fried in conch fritters

- ⓢ **Fried fish**

- ⓢ **Grouper**, a large fish caught in the waters just offshore, also appears on every menu

- ⓢ **Jerk** – pork, chicken, or fish – is marinated with a fiery mixture of spices, including hot Scotch bonnet peppers, pimento or allspice, nutmeg, escallion, and thyme

- ⓢ **Afungi**, a pudding of cornmeal and okra

- ⓢ **Breadfruit** – similar in taste to a potato, and served in as many ways

- ⓢ **Christophine**, a type of squash

- ⓢ **Dasheen** (a root vegetable similar to a potato)

- ⓢ **Fried plantains** (a non-sweet vegetable that resembles a banana).

- ⓢ **Peas** (usually red beans or pigeon peas) and rice: the number-one side dish in the Caribbean

Staying Happy & Healthy

Food & Drink

Stomach problems from food and water are at a minimum in the Caribbean. Most stomach distress is caused, not by the food itself, but by larger-than-usual amounts of food (combined, for many vacationers, with large amounts of rum).

Sunburn

Nothing will put a kink in a vacation any faster than a sunburn, your biggest danger in the Caribbean. You'll be surprised, even if you don't burn easily or if you already have a good base tan, at how easily the sun will sneak up on you. At this southern latitude, good sunscreen, applied liberally and often, is a must.

Insects

Oh, those pesky bugs! While the number of mosquitoes are generally fewer than in the American South (the omnipresent sea breeze keeps them at bay), the worst insects in the Caribbean are sand fleas. Popularly known as no-see-'ums, these critters raise itchy welts where they bite, usually along the ankles. Use an insect repellent if you'll be on the beach near sunset, the worst time of day for these unwelcome beach bums.

Manchineel Trees

Manchineel trees (*Hippomane mancinella*) present an unusual danger. These plants, members of the spurge plant family, have highly acidic leaves and fruit. During a rain, water dropping off the leaves can leave painful burns on your skin, and the trees' tiny apples will also burn when stepped on. In most resorts, manchineel trees have been removed or are clearly marked, often with signs and with trunks painted red.

Marine Dangers

For the two of us, a trip to the Caribbean isn't complete without snorkeling. While some inhabitants of the waters here look scary, most pose little danger. Exceptions are the ugly **scorpionfish** (a mottled pinkish fish that hangs out on coral and imparts a dangerous venom if touched or stepped on); **sea urchins** (painful if you step on their brittle spines); **jellyfish** (cause painful stings with their tentacles); and **stingrays** (dangerous if stepped on, they can be avoided by dragging your feet when wading). There are many varieties of **fire coral,** all edged in white. This coral will burn you to defend itself if you brush against it.

The best precaution is to follow your mother's advice: look but don't touch.

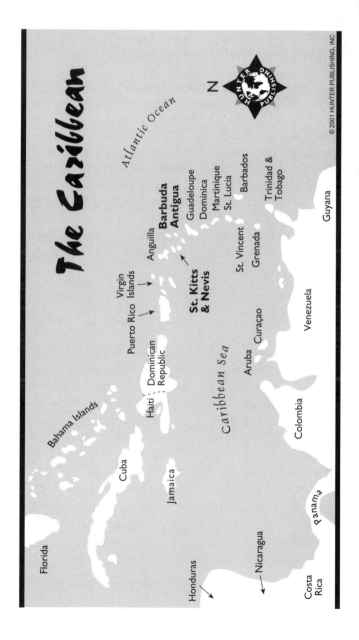

The Caribbean

Florida

Bahama Islands

Cuba

Jamaica

Haiti

Dominican Republic

Puerto Rico

Virgin Islands

Anguilla

Barbuda

Antigua

Guadeloupe

Dominica

Martinique

St. Lucia

Barbados

St. Vincent

Grenada

Trinidad & Tobago

Caribbean Sea

St. Kitts & Nevis

Aruba

Curaçao

Venezuela

Colombia

Guyana

Honduras

Nicaragua

Costa Rica

Panama

Atlantic Ocean

N

HUNTER PUBLISHING

© 2001 HUNTER PUBLISHING, INC

Nuts & Bolts

Getting Ready

When to Visit

The peak (read that as most expensive) time to visit the islands is winter or mid-December through mid-April. This is the busiest time of year, a season when Americans and Canadians are looking for a warm-weather refuge, if only for a few days, and when hotels and condominiums can charge peak prices.

You'll find equally pleasant weather conditions in the "shoulder" seasons – fall and spring. Prices are somewhat lower during these months and reservations are easier to obtain.

Summer months are the cheapest – look for rooms at 40% (sometimes even 50%) off of their peak rates. Early summer is especially pleasant. Late summer can bring hurricanes, but even that's a minor threat. Good forecasting systems keep travelers aware of any impending storms days in advance.

Entry Requirements

To gain entry to the islands, US and Canadian citizens need to show proof of citizenship in the form of a passport, or other proof of citizenship such as a birth certificate. Visitors must also show a return airline ticket.

Customs Regulations

For US Citizens

When you return to the US, you will pass through US Customs at your point of US entry. You'll complete a customs declaration form, one per household, identifying the total amount of your expenditures while out of the country. Each person has an exemption of US $400. A 10% tax is charged on the next $1,000 worth of goods. You may mail home gifts of up to $50 without duty and you may also take back one liter of wine or liquor and five cartons of cigarettes duty free.

Your duty-free allowance includes any items purchased in duty-free shops, gifts presented to you, gifts you bought in the islands for other people, and purchases you might be wearing, such as clothing or jewelry.

The US Department of Agriculture allows you to bring back up to one ounce of decorative beach sand.

Some items cannot be brought back to the US. These include:

- 🌀 books or cassettes made without authorized copyright ("pirated" copies)
- 🌀 any type of drug paraphernalia
- 🌀 firearms
- 🌀 fruits and vegetables
- 🌀 meats and their by-products (such as pâté)
- 🌀 plants, cuttings
- 🌀 tortoiseshell jewelry or other turtle products

> **🌀 AUTHOR'S TIP**
>
> To make your passage through Customs a little easier, keep your sales slips and pack so your purchases can be reached easily.

Before your trip, get a copy of the *Know Before You Go* brochure (Publication 512) from the US Customs Service at the airport or by contacting the US Customs Service, PO Box 7407, Washington, DC 20044; www.customs.ustreas.gov.

Canadian Citizens

If you are a Canadian citizen, you can return home with C $300 in goods duty free if you have been away from Canada for seven days or longer. This exemption is good once per year. If you've been away more than 48 hours but less than seven days, you can claim an additional exemption of C $100 per calendar quarter. (You can't claim the yearly and the quarterly exemptions within the same quarter.)

For UK Citizens

UK citizens can take home no more than 200 cigarettes or 100 cigarillos or 50 cigars (or 250 grams of tobacco) without duty; two liters of table wine; 50 grams of perfume or 60 cc and 250 cc of toilet water; and other goods up to a total of £145 (including gifts).

Passports

Obtaining a US Passport

To obtain a US passport, you may apply in person at the nearest passport office (see chart) or at one of the several thousand federal or state courts or US post offices authorized to accept passport applications. Not every post office will accept passport applications; it's usually one of the largest offices in the city. For your first passport application, you must apply in person.

We can't stress enough the importance of applying for a passport early. The heaviest demand period is January through August (because of summer travel), with September through December being the period with the quickest turnaround time. Even during the latter, however, you should allow at least eight weeks for your passport application to be processed.

To obtain a passport, first get an unsigned passport application (DSP-11) from your local passport office or post office that handles passport applications. You can also download a form online, http://travel.state.gov./passport_obtain.html. Do not sign the application.

Provide proof of US citizenship. This can be an expired passport, or a certified birth certificate (that means one with a raised, impressed, embossed, or multicolored seal). If you do not have a certified copy of your birth certificate, call the Bureau of Vital Statistics in the city where you were born. You also must provide identification, which could be an expired passport, a valid driver's license, a government ID card, or certificate of naturalization or citizenship. (Here's what won't work: Social Security card, learner's permit, temporary driver's license, credit card, expired ID card.)

Next, provide two identical photographs of yourself no larger than 2x2 inches (the image of your head from the bottom of your chin to the top of your head must not be less than one inch or more than 1⅜ inch). Passport photos can be either color or black and white, but they may not be Polaroids or vending machine photos. The easiest way to get passport photos is to go to one of the quick-copy stores and ask for passport shots.

Passports for adults 18 and over are $65 and are valid for 10 years. You may pay in person by check, bank draft, or money order. At passport agencies you may also pay in cash; some (but not all) post offices and court clerks accept payment in cash.

When you receive your passport, sign it. The next step is to fill in your address and a contact in case of emergency. A page is provided specifically for this purpose.

Need to talk with someone? The only public phone number for passport information is to the National Passport Information Center (NPIC). You can call here for information on passport emergencies, applying for a US passport, or to obtain the status of a passport application. Automated information is available 24 hours a day and live operators can be reached on workdays from 8 am to 8 pm, Eastern Standard Time. (Services are available in English, Spanish, and by TDD.) This is a toll call; the charge is 35 cents per minute for the automated system or $1.05 per minute for live operators. Call ☎ (900) 225-5674 for either automated or live service; or ☎ (900) 225-7778 for TDD service. Calling from a number blocked from 900 service? Call ☎ (888) 362-8668, TDD ☎ (888) 498-3648; you will be required to pay by credit card at a flat rate of $4.95 per call.

US Passport Offices

Boston Passport Agency
Thomas P. O'Neill Federal Building
10 Causeway Street, Room 247
Boston, MA 02222-1094
☎ (617) 565-6990

Region: Maine, Massachusetts, New Hampshire, Rhode Island, upstate New York, and Vermont

Chicago Passport Agency
Kluczynski Federal Building
230 S. Dearborn Street, Suite 380
Chicago, IL 60604-1564
☎ (312) 341-6020
Region: Illinois, Indiana, Michigan, and Wisconsin

Honolulu Passport Agency
First Hawaiian Tower
1132 Bishop Street, Suite 500
Honolulu, HI 96813-2809
☎ (808) 522-8283 or 522-8286
Region: American Samoa, Federated States of Micronesia, Guam, Hawaii, and Northern Mariana Islands

Houston Passport Agency
Mickey Leland Federal Building
1919 Smith Street, Suite 1100
Houston, TX 77002-8049
☎ (713) 209-3153
Region: Kansas, Oklahoma, New Mexico, and Texas

Los Angeles Passport Agency
Federal Building
11000 Wilshire Boulevard
Los Angeles, CA 90024-3615
☎ (310) 235-7070
Region: California (all counties south of and including San Luis Obispo, Kern, and

Nuts & Bolts

San Bernardino), and Nevada (Clark County only)

Miami Passport Agency
Claude Pepper Federal Office Building
51 SW First Avenue, 3rd Floor
Miami, FL 33120-1680
☎ (305) 536-4681
Region: Florida, Georgia, Puerto Rico, South Carolina, and US Virgin Islands

National Passport Center
31 Rochester Avenue
Portsmouth, NH 03801-2900
Applications handled: Applications for Passport by Mail (Form DSP-82) and workload transfers from regional passport agencies

New Orleans Passport Agency
Postal Services Building
701 Loyola Avenue, Suite T-12005
New Orleans, LA 70113-1931
☎ (504) 589-6161 or 589-6728, ext. 620
Region: Alabama, Arkansas, Iowa, Kentucky, Louisiana, Mississippi, Missouri, North Carolina, Ohio, Tennessee, and Virginia (except DC suburbs)

New York Passport Agency
376 Hudson Street
New York, NY 10014
☎ (212) 206-3500
Region: New York City and Long Island
Note: The New York Passport Agency accepts emergency applications only from

those leaving the country within two weeks.

Philadelphia Passport Agency
US Custom House
200 Chestnut Street, Room 103
Philadelphia, PA 19106-2970
☎ (215) 597-7480
Region: Delaware, New Jersey, Pennsylvania, and West Virginia

San Francisco Passport Agency
95 Hawthorne Street, 5th Floor
San Francisco, CA 94105
☎ (415) 974-4444 or 974-4010
Region: Arizona, California (all counties north of and including Monterey, Kings, Oulare, and Inyo), Nevada (except Clark Co.), and Utah

Seattle Passport Agency
915 Second Avenue, Suite 992
Seattle, WA 98174-1091
☎ (206) 220-7788
Region: Alaska, Colorado, Idaho, Minnesota, Montana, Nebraska, North Dakota, Oregon, South Dakota, Washington, and Wyoming

Stamford Passport Agency
One Landmark Square
Broad and Atlantic Streets
Stamford, CT 06901-2667
☎ (203) 325-3530
Region: Connecticut & Westchester County (New York)

Nuts & Bolts

Washington Passport Agency
1111 19th Street, N.W.
Washington, D.C. 20524
☎ (202) 647-0518
Region: Maryland, Northern Virginia (including Alexandria, Arlington County, and Fairfax County), and the District of Columbia

Special Issuance Agency
1111 19th Street, N.W. Room 300
Washington, D.C. 20522-1705
Contact this office if your application needs special attention.

 # Packing to Go

We're happy to say that you won't need to pack a steamer trunk for a vacation in the islands. No matter what your planned activities, you'll find that these are fairly casual islands, with shorts and T-shirts being the uniform during the day. Be sure to bring along at least two swimsuits (the high humidity means that clothing takes extra time to dry) and cover-ups. Swimwear is appropriate only at the beach so you will want a cover-up, no matter how casual, for lunches and quick excursions.

Evenings are more dressy, especially during high season. With their strong British heritage and large number of UK visitors, these islands follow a more conservative dress code when it comes to evening wear. Jackets are par for the course at many of the small inns.

We do recommend a few items for all visitors:

- ❏ *proof of citizenship*
- ❏ *airline tickets*
- ❏ *snorkel, fins, and mask*
- ❏ *sunscreen*
- ❏ *aloe vera gel*
- ❏ *first-aid kit*
- ❏ *cameras, flash, and film (we recommend an inexpensive underwater camera as well)*
- ❏ *driver's license for car rental*
- ❏ *swimsuit*
- ❏ *all prescriptions (in prescription bottles)*
- ❏ *mini-address book*

Nuts & Bolts

If you'll be scuba diving, don't forget your "C" card as well as any gear you typically bring along such as a compass, dive tables, dive computer, weight belt, mesh bag, dive boots, logbook, and proof of insurance. Anyone considering a boat excursion should bring along some non-skid shoes as well.

A good rule of thumb for packing is to pack completely and then remove one third of your items.

Making Plans

Air-Land Package Deals

Several airlines offer package deals that provide for a complete vacation: room, transfers, air, and, for all-inclusives, meals, drinks, and tips. Is this cheaper than putting a package together on your own? Usually. Check it out for yourself by calling the hotel reservation numbers, asking for their room rate and adding it to the cost of an airline ticket. You'll usually see a substantial savings, since, after all, the airlines are buying rooms in bulk and therefore have much more purchasing power than an ordinary consumer.

Some travelers worry about the term "package," imagining a trip where they'll be herded on a tour bus with a hundred other tourists. Have no fear. Some packages include the services of a greeter at the airport who will welcome you and show you the way to the transfer bus to your hotel, but beyond that you're on your own. If you want to rent a car and explore, go for it.

Packages are also offered by charter airlines, which offer service at a lower cost, usually with few frills. (Often only one class of service is available, seat assignments are given only at check-in, and carry-on allowances may be only one bag per passenger due to an increased number of seats onboard.) Ask your travel agent for information on charters available from your area.

If you don't want the package vacation, some of these charters also sell "air-only," which is just the airline tickets themselves.

FREQUENT FLYER PROGRAMS

When you purchase your airline ticket, sign up for the airline's frequent flyer program. Also, check to see if your resort is part of the frequent flyer program. For instance, Sandals (see page 53) offers American Airlines frequent flyer miles for every night's stay.

Today you can earn mileage in many ways other than flying. Long distance companies, credit card companies, dining programs, and others offer miles, sometimes as many as five for every dollar spent.

Travel Between Islands

Want to island-hop? It's fun and, if you're visiting small islands, a necessary part of a Caribbean vacation.

Two carriers offer special passes designed for island hopping. **LIAT**, ☎ (800) 468-0482, and **BWIA**, ☎ (800) 327-7401, each offer a special pass that permits you to hop from island to island, with certain restrictions. We took LIAT's **Explorer's Pass**, a US $199 bargain, and made three island stops within a 21-day limit. The catch is that you must make all of your travel in one direction, except for the return flight back to the island from which you started. These passes must be purchased and ticketed (a very important detail) within the continental US. They cannot be purchased in the Caribbean.

When traveling on these small carriers, be prepared to carry on only one small bag. You'll be able to check in other luggage either at the ticket counter or right at the airplane door as you board (our choice, so we can make sure the bags board the same plane we do).

Service may be limited on some flights. A few times we have flown on prop planes when the only staff members were the pilot and co-pilot, seated just a couple of seats ahead of us. The flights are generally short, though, and really give you a bird's-eye view of the islands that can't be beat.

Check-in requirements are upheld stringently with the small carriers. Some flights have been known to leave early, so make sure that you check in ahead of schedule. Call the night before and re-confirm your seats, then arrive at the airport at the stated check-in time.

Using Travel Agents

Travel agents offer a generally free service, making hotel and air reservations and issuing airline tickets (although some agents are now charging for certain services). They can shop around for the lowest rate for you and often know about sales that aren't available to the general public.

They can't, however, read your mind. We've seen vacationers go to a travel agent and say "We'd like to go somewhere warm." That covers a lot of territory!

Every vacation is a once-in-a-lifetime opportunity. You may return to the islands, but no other trip will be exactly like this one. Each is unique and offers wonderful opportunities for you to explore the world.

Part of the fun of travel is the anticipation of the trip. Read this book. Go by the travel agent's office and pick up some brochures. Rent some travel videos. Talk about your options.

When you have your minds made up – or at least narrowed down – return to the travel agent for some help. If it's a large office, ask for an agent who specializes in the Caribbean.

Nuts & Bolts

General Information

Climate

St. Kitts and Nevis enjoy an average temperature of 79°. Average rainfall is 55 inches (but higher in the rain forest areas).

Temperatures range from 76° in the winter months to 85° in the summer in Antigua and Barbuda. There is an average of 40 inches of rainfall per year.

Hurricanes

Mention weather and the Caribbean in the same sentence and, quite predictably, the topic of hurricanes arises. These deadly storms are officially a threat from June through November, although the greatest danger is during the later months, basically August through October (September is the worst).

Hurricanes are defined as revolving storms with wind speeds of 75 mph or greater. These counter-clockwise storms begin as waves off the west coast of Africa and work their way across the Atlantic, some eventually gaining strength and becoming tropical depressions (under 40 mph) or tropical storms (40-74 mph). Excellent warning systems keep islanders posted of the possibility of oncoming storms. While on these islands, tune in to Radio ZIZ, 555AM, for weather bulletins.

Beat the Heat

In the Caribbean the mercury regularly rises above 90° on summer days. In these conditions, you'll need to take extra precautions to make sure you don't fall ill.

The first concern is heat cramps, which are muscle cramps caused because of water and salt loss through perspiration. From there, it's not far to heat exhaustion, when the body tries to cool itself off and the victim feels, well, exhausted and even nauseous. Finally, heat stroke can set in, a life-threatening condition.

What can you do to avoid these conditions?

 ☺ First, drink water, lots of water. Don't wait until you're thirsty to reach for the water jug. Thirst is an early sign of heat stress, so start drinking before it reaches that point.

- ⊚ Slow down. Curtail your activities whenever possible and do like the animals do in the high heat – move slowly.

- ⊚ Take lots of breaks if excercising out of doors.

- ⊚ Stay out of the direct sun.

- ⊚ Make sure you are well protected from the sun. Wear wide-brimmed hats and caps as well as sunglasses.

- ⊚ Wear sunscreen. Sunburned skin is a definite no-no.

- ⊚ Avoid being outside between 10 am and 2 pm, when the sun's rays are the strongest. Enjoy an early morning hike, then kick back and take a swim break that afternoon.

Credit Cards

Major credit cards are accepted at most establishments on these islands.

Crime

Take the usual precautions you would exercise at home, especially on the larger and somewhat more congested Antigua.

Nuts & Bolts

Drugs

Be warned that these islands exercise strict anti-drug laws. Marijuana is an illegal substance and possession of it can result not only in large fines but also in a prison term.

Electrical Current

Dual voltage of 220 and 110 AC, 60 cycles is available in some hotels; converters from 220 to 110 are widely available.

Immunizations

No immunizations are required to travel to these islands.

Language

English, with a West Indian lilt, is spoken throughout the islands.

Money Matters

The Eastern Caribbean dollar (EC) is used throughout Antigua and Barbuda and St. Kitts and Nevis. The fixed exchange rate is US $1 to EC $2.68.

CURRENCY CONVERSION CHART

US DOLLARS (rounded up for easy conversion)

US $ to EC $		EC $ to US $	
$1	$2.70	$1	37¢
$5	$13.50	$5	$1.87
$10	$27.00	$10	$3.74
$25	$67.50	$25	$9.36
$50	$135.00	$50	$18.72
$75	$202.50	$75	$27.78
$100	$270.00	$100	$37.00

CANADIAN DOLLARS

CA $ to EC $		EC $ to CA $	
$1	$1.82	$1	$1.10
$5	$9.10	$5	$2.74
$10	$18.21	$10	$5.49
$25	$45.52	$25	$13.72
$50	$91.05	$50	$27.44
$75	$136.50	$75	$41.25
$100	$182.00	$100	$55.00

BRITISH POUNDS

£ to EC $		EC $ to £	
$1	$4.06	$1	25 pence
$5	$20.28	$5	$1.23
$10	$40.57	$10	$2.46
$25	$101.42	$25	$6.16
$50	$202.84	$50	$12.32
$75	$304.50	$75	$18.75
$100	$406.00	$100	$25.00

Nuts & Bolts

Photography

Ask permission before taking photos of people. In some of the market areas you will be expected to make a purchase before taking a photo.

Telephones

There is some direct calling service to the US from Antigua and Barbuda as well as St. Kitts and Nevis. If direct service is not available, your hotel can transfer you to an operator who will connect you.

Time Zone

These islands are on Atlantic Standard Time, which is one hour ahead of Eastern Standard Time.

Tipping

Standard tips are 10-15%, although some hotels and restaurants will add 10% gratuity automatically. Bellmen usually receive 50¢ per bag, and taxi drivers get 10-15% of the fare.

Water

Water is safe to drink on all the islands.

Antigua & Barbuda

A Capsule History

The First Inhabitants

Pre-colonial Antigua was originally inhabited by the Siboney ("stone people" in the Arawak language) Indians, whose hand-crafted shell and stone tools have been found at archaeological sites around the island. Some of these artifacts have been dated back to 1775 BC.

The next inhabitants of Antigua were the Arawak Indians, moving in about AD 35 and living here until about AD 1100. These farmers were overthrown by the warlike Caribs, a people known for their cannibalism. The Caribs named the island **Wadadli** (today, that's the name of the local beer).

Colonization

In 1493, Christopher Columbus named the island in honor of Santa Maria de La Antigua of Seville, a saint at whose namesake church Columbus had prayed before his journey to the Americas. Even after European discovery, however, things stayed quiet here for a century, mostly due to the fierce Caribs and the island's lack of fresh water.

In 1632, an English party from St. Kitts landed on Antigua and claimed it for Britain, starting a relationship that endured nearly 350 years. In 1981, Antigua and Barbuda gained their full independence.

When European settlement began, Antigua was developed as a sugar-producing island and English Harbour became a home base for the British naval fleet. Admiral Horatio Nelson, Britain's greatest naval hero, directed his campaigns from the Dockyard at English Harbour.

In 1834, slavery was abolished and the sugar industry faltered. A century later, it was replaced by the development of the tourism industry.

Independence

In 1967, Antigua became the first of the Eastern Caribbean countries to attain internal self government as a state in association with Great Britain as part of the West Indies Act. Full independence was achieved on November 1, 1981.

Timeline

1775 BC - Occupation of island by Siboney Indians.

35 - Occupation of island by Arawak Indians.

1100 - Overthrow of the island by Carib Indians.

1493 - European discovery by Christopher Columbus.

1632 - Antigua claimed for Great Britain.

1834 - Slavery was abolished.

1967 - Antigua attained internal self government.

1981 - Antigua achieved full independence.

The People

The two islands have a combined population of about 67,000. Most residents are of African descent, with the remainder being of British, Lebanese, Syrian, and Portuguese origin.

Environment

Antigua is located in the middle of the **Leeward Islands**, about 300 miles southeast of Puerto Rico or 1,300 miles southeast of Miami. The island is the largest of the Leewards, with 108 square miles.

Antigua is a limestone and coral island, somewhat scrubby with rolling hills, especially on the southern reaches. The highest point is **Boggy Peak** (1,330 feet). The capital city is **St. John's**, home to most of the tourist shopping and the cruise port. The south shore of the island is favored by yachties, who call into **Nelson's Dockyard** at **English Harbour**.

Barbuda lies 27 miles northeast of Antigua and covers 62 square miles. It's best known for its pink sand beaches. **Redonda**, an uninhabited island that forms the third piece of this nation, lies 20 miles to the west.

Flora

The national flower of Antigua and Barbuda is the **dagger log** (*Agave karatto*). A member of the lily family, this tall plant with dagger-like leaves can reach about 20 feet. It blooms only once in its lifetime, and after the bloom the entire plant dies. The dagger log has been used for many purposes through the years, from fiber for robes to medicine for tuberculosis.

The national fruit is the **Antigua black pineapple** (*Ananas comosus*). The Arawak Indians first brought this fruit to the islands from South America.

Birds

Many species of birds can be found in Antigua and Barbuda. Bird-watchers enjoy the **Frigate Bird Sanctuary** on Barbuda (see page 111). Housing over 170 species, it is the largest bird sanctuary in the Caribbean. There are also several other places on the islands where tropical birds can be spotted.

Life Undersea

The marine life in this area is some of the richest in the Caribbean. Gorgonians, barrel sponges, tube sponges, and other colorful formations make the experience extraordinary for even the most experienced divers.

Besides the coral and colorful fish that live in the formations, it is always a treat, though not an uncommon one, to see a **Southern Atlantic stingray.** This is the most common type of stingray. They're found in shallow bays near the sandy bottoms where they feed on mollusks and crustaceans. Stingrays are considered a choice meal by sharks, and have a barbed tail for protection. Like a scorpion's tail, the barb is brought up to defend the ray from attack from above. These rays are either a dark gray or brown with a white belly. They can reach up to six feet in width.

The **green sea turtle** is found along the Atlantic, Gulf of Mexico, Mediterranean, Pacific, and Indian Oceans and can often be spotted in the waters of Antigua and Barbuda. These turtles have been observed to remain underwater for several days without surfacing for air as they seek food. Even in their current protected state, it's not an easy life; only one turtle out of 10,000 eggs laid reaches maturity. The hazards are many: birds, animals, marine life, humans. You name it, it's a threat to these little guys. Nevertheless, the turtle has continued to thrive.

> ### ⚡ WARNING!
>
> Whenever you are snorkeling or diving, watch out for fire coral. There are many varieties, but all are edged in white. If you accidentally brush against the coral it will defend itself and burn you like fire!

Getting Here

By Air

Most visitors arrive in Antigua at **V.C. Bird International Airport**, on the island's northeast corner. (Once on Antigua, there are several ways to reach Barbuda; these are outlined below.) V.C. Bird airport is served by flights from the US and Europe and is also a bustling hub for airlines such as **LIAT** for many inter-island flights.

Air service from North America is available from:

Air Canada . . . . ☎ (888) 358-2262
www.aircanada.com
American Airlines . . . ☎ (800) 433-7300
www.aa.com

BWIA . . . . ☎ (800) JET-BWIA (US)
www.bwee.com/caribbean

Continental Airlines. . . ☎ (800) 231-0856
www.continental.com

Inter-island air service is available from:

LIAT. . . . . ☎ (268) 462-0700

Air St. Kitts/Nevis. . . . ☎ (268) 465-8571
(call collect)

Carib Aviation. . . . . . . ☎ (268) 462-3147

Approximate Flight Times

Dallas.	5½ hours
Los Angeles	8½ hours
Miami	2¼ hours
New York. . . . . , ...	3½ hours
Toronto . . . . , ...	4½ hours

It's a quick 15-minute flight from Antigua to Barbuda. You'll find guided day trips available from several tour operators in Antigua (see Barbuda chapter, below) or you can also book with **Carib Airlines** (☎ 869-465-3055, www.candoo.com/carib). The smaller airlines listed above offer charter flights to the island. Planes are small, carrying four, five, or seven passengers.

Another option is to arrive on Barbuda via powerboat. The 1½-hour trip from Antigua is offered by **Adventure Antigua** (☎ 268-727-3261 or 268-560-4672, www.adventureantigua.com, e-mail adventureantigua@yahoo.co.uk). This day trip departs the west coast of Antigua early in the morning for a day of snorkeling and exploring in Barbuda, along with a visit to the bird sanctuary. Tours cost US $150 per person.

US, Canadian, and UK vacationers must show either a passport or a birth certificate and photo ID as well as an onward or return ticket. The departure tax is US $12.

By Cruise Ship

 Antigua is a popular destination for many cruise ships. Two cruise terminals, approximately two miles apart, are in downtown St. John's and are within walking distance of the main shopping areas. One is adjacent to **Heritage Quay** duty-free shopping center and the other is at **Deep Water**.

The following cruise lines sometimes stop in Antigua:

Cunard Lines . . . . ☎ 800-7-CUNARD
www.cunard.com
Holland-America . . . . . . ☎ (800) 426-0327
www.hollandamerica.com
Clipper Cruise Line . . . . ☎ (800) 325-0100
www.clippercruise.com
Carnival Cruises ☎ (800) 888-CARNIVAL
www.carnivalcruise.com
Royal Caribbean . . . . ☎ (888) 313-8883
www.royalcaribbean.com

Princess Cruises. . . . . ☎ (800) PRINCESS
www.princesscruises.com
Celebrity Cruises . . . . . . ☎ (888) 313-8883
www.celebrity-cruises.com
Fred Olsen Cruises . . . . ☎ (01473) 292222
Royal Olympic . . . . ☎ (800) 872-6400
UK (0171) 7340805

By Private Boat

Private boats can enter Antigua through
English Harbour (☎ 268-460-7979); and
the **St. James' Club** (☎ 268-460-5000),
both on the south coast Other marinas include **St. John's Harbour** (west) and
Crabbs Marina (northeast).

Inter-Island Travel

There are several ways to island-hop
while you're in Antigua and Barbuda. The
most common is to charter a flight with
any of these companies, which fly to most
of the nearby islands.

LIAT . . . . ☎ (268) 462-0700
Air St. Kitts/Nevis . . . ☎ (268) 465-8571
Carib Aviation . . . . . . ☎ (268) 462-3147

EMBASSIES & CONSULATES

Run into problems on your trip? You will find consulates and embassies on some of the larger islands. These offices can assist you with lost or stolen passports, emergencies, etc.

If you lose your passport or have it stolen, first report the loss to the local police. Get a Police Declaration and then report to the consul for a replacement passport. We've had this happen and relied on the State Department to help us replace a lost passport (caused by the sinking of a boat we were traveling in) with an emergency passport. We can't emphasize enough how important it is to carry a copy of the identification page of your passport tucked somewhere in your belongings. We didn't then, but we always carry this with us now.

If you are involved in an emergency situation, go to the US embassy or consular office and register. Bring along your passport and a location where you can be reached.

The consular office can also be contacted for a list of local doctors, dentists, and medical specialists. If you are injured or become seriously ill, a consul will help you find medical assistance and, at your request, inform your family or friends. The

State Department cannot assist you in funding an emergency trip back to the States – that's what travel insurance is all about.

American Consular Agent
Hospital Hill, Nelson's Dockyard PO
English Harbour, Antigua
☎ (268) 460-1569

Getting Ready

Sources of Information

Tourism Offices

For materials on Antigua and Barbuda, including maps, brochures, and rate sheets, contact the Antigua and Barbuda Department of Tourism closest to you.

Antigua & Barbuda Dept.
of Tourism & Trade
25 S.E. 2nd Avenue, Suite 300
Miami, FL 33131
☎ (305) 381-6762; fax (305) 381-7908

Antigua & Barbuda Dept. of Tourism
610 Fifth Avenue, Suite 311
New York, NY 10020
☎ (212) 541-4117; fax (212) 514-4789

Antigua & Barbuda Dept.
of Tourism & Trade
60 St. Claire Avenue East, Suite 304
Toronto, Ontario
Canada M4T 1N5
☎ (416) 961-3085; fax (416) 961-7218

On-Island Information

Antigua & Barbuda Dept. of Tourism
Nevis Street and Friendly Avenue
PO Box 363
St. John's, Antigua, West Indies
☎ (268) 462-0480; fax (268) 462-2483

For materials on hotels, condominiums, and resorts, contact:

Antigua Hotels &
Tourists Association
PO Box 454
St. John's, Antigua, West Indies
☎ (268) 462-0374; fax 268-462-3702

Internet Information

Another good source of information is the Internet. Visit **www.antigua-barbuda.org**.

Once You Arrive

Credit Cards

Major credit cards are accepted everywhere on the island.

Newspapers/Broadcast Media

The local newspapers are an excellent way to keep up with island activities and to get some insight into life beyond the resorts and hotels.

Daily Observer, St. John's, ☎ (268) 480-1750

Sentinel Newspaper, St. John's, ☎ (268) 462-5500

Antigua Sun, St. John's, ☎ (268) 480-5960

Telephones

There is some direct calling service from Antigua and Barbuda. If there is no service available, your hotel can transfer you to an operator who will connect you.

Culture & Customs

What to Expect

Antigua and Barbuda have a West Indian atmosphere and feel. With a long history of British rule, there is a slightly more formal atmosphere in personal relations – people are often introduced as Mr. or Ms. Also, as in most of the Caribbean, it's traditional to greet others with a "Good morning" or "Good afternoon" and a smile, rather than just launching into your question or request.

Language

English is the primary language in Antigua and Barbuda, and it is spoken with a distinct West Indian lilt. Although English is the official language, you will quickly notice that it follows British, not American, spellings, such as colour, travellers, and centre.

Holidays

The hottest event of the year is **Antigua Sailing Week**, held in April. During this time, Antigua hotel rooms can be hard to come by. (See below for event description.)

Another special event is **Independence Day** on November 1st. **Carnival** is the hottest summer activity, scheduled in late July to commemorate emancipation. The events include steel pan music, calypso, beauty pageants, and parades with elaborately costumed musicians in bands of 75 to 300 members. Join in the fun and march with the musical troupes as they wind their way through St. John's. You'll find plenty of local food at **Carnival City** (otherwise known as the Antigua Recreation Grounds in St. John's): seasoned rice, doucana (a dumpling made of flour, sweet potatoes, coconut, and sometimes raisins), and saltfish.

In late October and early November, the **Hot Air Balloon Festival** lights the skies (see below).

Public holidays on both islands are:

New Year's Day . . . . January 1
Good Friday . . . . . . variable, as in the US
Easter Monday . . . . variable, as in the US
Labour Day . . . . May 5
Whit Monday . . . . late May; variable
Caricom Day . . . . July 7
Independence Day . . . . November 1
Christmas Day . . . . December 25
Boxing Day . . . . December 26

⊙ **TIP**

For more information on any of the local festivities listed below, call the Department of Tourism, ☎ (268) 462-0480.

☀ JANUARY

Antigua Winter Windsurfing Competition

Course and slalom racing at Lord Nelson Beach. For entry requirements, contact the Tourism office.

☀ FEBRUARY

Antigua Grand Prix Regatta, *Jolly Harbour*

This event features seven short yacht races. ☎ (268) 460-7468.

☀ APRIL

Antigua Sailing Week, *Antigua*

Throughout the week, Nelson's Dockyard at English Harbour comes to life with the color and pageantry of the largest regatta in the Caribbean. Parties, barbecues, races, Lord Nelson's Ball and more highlight this annual event, now in its third decade. ☎ (268) 462-8872.

Dept. of Tourism Model Boat Race

(pre-Sailing Week), Antigua

Models are shown and raced by their owners and builders. ☎ (268) 463-0125.

☀ MAY

Curtain Bluff Hotel Pro-Am Tennis Classic,

near Carlisle Bay

Tennis pros offer lessons and play matches. Call the hotel for times and ticket information. ☎ (268) 462-8400.

Liberation Day Rally*, St. John's*
Celebrates African Liberation Day. The event is
sponsored by the local Rastafarian community.

Labour Day*, Antigua & Barbuda*
This public holiday is marked with picnics and
beach fun.

☀ JUNE

Caribuna*, Barbuda*
This carnival features local foods and all the fun
and color of a traditional Caribbean "jump-up," or
party. Live music. ☎ (268) 460-0077.

☀ JULY

Carib Cup Regatta*, Jolly Harbour, Antigua*
This Antigua-to-Barbuda yacht race is always
well attended. For participation information,
☎ (268) 460-7468.

☀ AUGUST

Antigua Carnival enlivens the month of August, and sometimes events start in late July.
Carnival Monday and Tuesday (dates vary) are
public holidays and these two days mark the
height of the celebrations.

☀ SEPTEMBER

Jolly Harbour Regatta*, Antigua*
Features four short yacht races. Held on the last
weekend of the month. ☎ (268) 462-6041.

☀ OCTOBER

International Hot Air Balloon Festival,
Antigua

Close to a dozen hot air balloons schedule launches at English Harbour, Newfield, Jolly Harbour, St. John's, Curtain Bluff, and other sites around the island. To celebrate Antigua's independence, British sky divers jump from 2,000 feet carrying the Antiguan flag. Other festivities include parades, gun salutes, and dancing in St. John's. A night flight over English Harbour makes for a spectacular scene. Enjoy this spectator event. ☎ (268) 462-0480.

Heritage (National Dress) Day, Antigua

Parades of costumed residents, decorated buildings. Late October, but general celebrations continue into May. ☎ (268) 462-0480.

☀ NOVEMBER

The International Hot Air Balloon Festival continues throughout the month of November.

Antigua Open Golf Tournament

This annual contest is open to both members and visitors. It takes place at the Cedar Valley Golf Club. ☎ (268) 462-0161.

Annual Sports Events

From September through December is basketball season. December-July is volleyball season. January-July brings cricketers out onto the field, while

August through February is football (soccer) season.

These spectator sports take place across the islands. If you're interested in watching (or even playing), contact the Department of Tourism, ☎ (268) 462-0480.

Weddings

Antigua and Barbuda are two of the simplest Caribbean islands on which to tie the knot. There is no waiting time, so you could fly in and get married that same afternoon.

On weekdays, bring your paperwork (proof of citizenship and, if applicable, a certified divorce decree or death certificate of previous spouse) to the Ministry of Justice in St. John's, sign a declaration before the Marriage Coordinator, and pay the EC $150 license fee. The Coordinator makes arrangements for a Marriage Officer to perform the civil ceremony. The Marriage Officer is also paid EC $50; payments can be made in US dollars. Those staying on Barbuda will need to travel to Antigua to take care of the paperwork.

One of the top resorts on Antigua for wedding ceremonies is **Sandals** (www.sandals.com, ☎ 888-SANDALS). Call or contact Sandals' wedding division for a wedding form and details. The **Wedding Moon** package includes preparation of documents, legal fees, minister or other officiating party, witnesses, wedding announcement cards, champagne and hors d'oeuvres, bouquet and boutonniere, Caribbean wedding cake, video of your ceremony, 5x7 photo, candlelight dinner for two, "just married" T-shirts, continental breakfast in bed the morning after the wedding, decorated wedding area, and taped musical accompaniment. Check with Sandals for the current fee; lately they've been offering the package free with stay. Additional services can be purchased and include manicure/pedicure, full body massage, hairstyling, make-up session in your room, personal dressing assistant, private car transfers to and from the airport, additional photos, "Sunset Hour" Moët and Chandon with hors d'oeuvres, private champagne/canape cruise, calypso band, guest day passes, floral decorations, and more.

 # The Attractions

Antigua

Antigua (pronounced an-TEE-ga) doesn't have the quaint shopping zones of islands like St. Martin or the lush tropical beauty of St. Kitts and Nevis.

What Antigua has are beaches: 365 of them, the tourism folks claim. Stretches of white sand that border turquoise waters teeming with marine life. Beaches where you can walk and hardly see another soul. Beaches where you can shop for local crafts and buy a burger at a beachside grill. And beaches where you can just curl up under a tall coconut palm and see the end of another Caribbean day, watching for the green flash as the sun sinks into the sea.

Antigua, which was battered by Hurricane Luis in 1995, is back to top condition. Some hotels were closed for refurbishments in the months following the storm, but most properties are up and running at full speed these days, sporting fresh facades with few indications that the island ever suffered such a terrible storm.

Barbuda

Barbuda's greatest is attraction is nature and the solitude that comes with it. Few islands are as quiet or as peaceful, and it's this that attracts people. It's a great spot for birders, and also has a number of spectacular beaches.

Fishing, golf, tennis, snorkeling, diving, and beachcombing are all available on this tiny island.

Antigua

Transportation

See pages 40-41 for details about airlines serving Antigua.

GETTING A DEAL ON YOUR FLIGHT

Shop around for tickets. Start early, be patient, and do some research. Check with several carriers, even those that aren't the primary airlines in your region. Chances are, unless you are starting from an East Coast hub, you'll be making connections along the way, so sometimes it pays to do some creative routing – although you will pay for it in travel time.

Getting Around the Island

Car & Jeep Rentals

You'll need to show a valid license (foreign or an international license) and provide a major credit card. Prices average about US $40 to $50 per day.

A temporary Antiguan driver's license is also required (US $12) and can be obtained at the airport or at any Antiguan police station. Some roads are

If you want to see much of the island, it pays to invest in a rental car.

a little bumpy, so if you plan to travel out away from the major destinations, we recommend you carry a spare tire. Also, try to fill up on gas before leaving the towns.

CAR RENTAL COMPANIES	
Anjam Rent-A-Car	☎ (268) 462-0959/2173
Avis Rent-A-Car	☎ (268) 462-2840/7
Budget Rent-A-Car	☎ (268) 462-3009
Dollar Rent-A-Car	☎ (268) 462-0362/0123
Hertz Rent-A-Car	☎ (268) 462-4114/5
J&L Rent-A-Car	☎ (268) 461-7496
Jonas Rent-A-Car	☎ (268) 462-3760
National Car Rental	☎ (268) 462-2113
Richard's Rent-A-Car	☎ (268) 462-0976
Supa Rentals	☎ (268) 462-7872

Driving Tips

Look right before crossing the street!

Traffic keeps to the left side of the road. This can be confusing on your first day behind the wheel, so start off a little slower than usual. Most cars are right-hand drive, which will also necessitate a few adjustments.

Scooters & Bicycles

Rent your vehicle of choice at **Shipwreck Rent-A-Scooter Bicycles-Motorbikes**, English Harbour, St. John's, ☎ (268) 460-6087/464-7771.

Taxis

Taxi travel is the most common means of transportation, especially for travelers not comfortable with driving on the left side of the road. Taxi fares from the St. John's area to Nelson's Dockyard on the far side of the island run about US $50, round trip. Here are some typical taxi fares:

```
Airport to Nelson's Dockyard . . . . US $21
Airport to Shirley Heights . . . . . . . US $21
Airport to St. John's . . . . . . . . . . . . US $7
```

Island Tours

Antigua's visitors often head to Barbuda on a day-trip. Tour prices of US $125 to $139 per person include round-trip air from Antigua, a sightseeing tour, a visit to the Frigate Bird Sanctuary and lunch. **LIAT** offers packages to Barbuda; for information, ☎ (800) 468-0482 or (800) 981-8585.

TOUR COMPANIES	
Antours, St. John's	☎ (268) 462-4788
Bo Tours, St. John's	☎ (268) 462-6632
Coral Island, St. John's	☎ (268) 460-5625
Discovery Tours, St. John's	☎ (268) 460-7478
Kiskidee Tours, St. John's	☎ (268) 480-8651

Antigua

Orientation

Antigua is sometimes described as amoeba-shaped. Lined with numerous inlets and bays, the coastline skirts in and out around the island.

Unlike some of the Leeward Islands, which are circled by a coastal road, Antigua's road system is based more on a hub system. Roads radiate out from the capital city of St. John's, on the northwest coast.

V.C. Bird International Airport is on the island's north-northeast coast. Located about 15 to 20 minutes from St. John's, this end of the island is fairly dry and scrubby, with low rolling hills covered by low-growing vegetation.

North of St. John's lies **Dickenson** and **Runaways bays**, both popular tourist destinations and known for their excellent beaches. West of St. John's lies **Hawksbill Bay**, home of an excellent resort of the same name with four picturesque beaches.

South of St. John's the roads fan out in various directions around the island. Various routes follow the coastline around **Green Castle Hill**; others take travelers to one of Antigua's top sites, **English Harbour**. Home of the historic **Nelson's Dockyard National Park**, this region is a favorite with eco-tourists and history buffs alike.

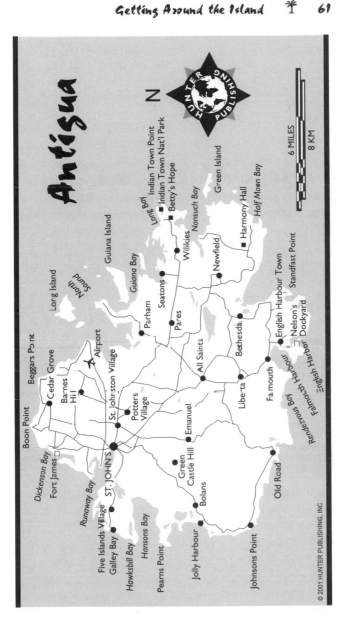

Antigua

East of St. John's, roads travel to **Betty's Hope**, an old sugar plantation, and on to the island's most rugged shores. Here, the Atlantic meets the land, creating beautiful vistas, choppy waters, and several interesting geological formations.

 **Best Places to Stay**

Room prices vary greatly with the type of accommodation, location, and time of year. High season (mid-December through mid-April) brings prices about 40% higher than in summer months.

The Alive! Price Scale

All prices are given in US dollars.

Deluxe	$300+
Expensive	$200-$300
Moderate	$100-$200
Inexpensive	Under $100

Resorts & Hotels

SANDALS ANTIGUA RESORT AND SPA
Dickenson Bay Road, 15 mins. north of St. John's
☎ (268) 462-0267; fax (268) 462-4135
Reservations: ☎ (800) SANDALS
www.sandals.com
Moderate-Expensive

Like the other couples-only resorts in this popular chain, Sandals Antigua offers an array of activities that can keep even the most restless vacationer happy. Activity coordinators, or "Playmakers," keep things going for those who want to stay busy. For couples preferring inactivity, two-person hammocks and "love baskets," swinging wicker baskets, offer quiet afternoons beneath shady palapas.

Unlike other Sandals, about half of the clientele at this resort is European. Most visitors are young couples, and, especially during the spring and summer months, many are honeymooners or couples getting married on their honeymoon. During our late May visit, we counted three weddings on one afternoon alone.

We liked this Sandals for its low-slung buildings spread along a wide swath of white beach. We stayed in a rondoval room, an octagon-shaped cabin with a tall conical ceiling, louvered windows, and a true Caribbean atmosphere. At this resort, guests in the upper category rooms enjoy Suite Concierge Service for booking restaurant reservations or assistance with island tours, a fully stocked, complimentary in-room bar, a daily *New York Times* fax, and terrycloth robes. Another romantic feature here is the excellent spa, although spa services are not part of the all-inclusive package.

Like other properties in this chain, the resort has many restaurants from which to choose: an open-air main dining room that offers international fare in the evenings served à la carte, an Italian restaurant (with an excellent sunset view – get there early for a beachside table), and a Japanese

Antigua

restaurant where active chefs will prepare your meal right at the table amid a flurry of flying knives and implements.

SANDALS' ISLAND HOPPER PROGRAM

Sandals resorts are recommended as one of the top accommodations for couples.

Sandals offers a unique "Island Hopper" program. The two of you can design a custom itinerary and hop from one Sandals to another. Air isn't included, but you can design your own package and change room categories from property to property if you like. Sandals resorts are found on Antigua, Jamaica (six properties), the Bahamas, and St. Lucia (two properties). Check out the Sandals Website at www.sandals.com or ask your travel agent for more details.

SUNSAIL COLONNA CLUB
Hodges Bay
St. John's Antigua, West Indies
Reservations: ☎ (800) 327-2276
www.sunsail.com
Inexpensive-Moderate

If you love the water and sailing, then you'll love Sunsail. This international company, with clubs as far away as Turkey, is a favorite among the sailing world. Here you'll find an array of vessels to take out and enjoy and, if you don't know stern from bow, you can take expert lessons here as well, all part of the all-inclusive plan.

Sunsail isn't fancy, but it is one of the best bargains in the Caribbean. All rooms are air conditioned and include satellite TV, telephone, mini refrigerator, and tea- and coffee-making facilities. There are numerous twin and double rooms as well as apartments and two- or three-bedroom villas.

But the real attraction here comes in the form of watersports. The resort hugs a small cove where instruction is available in dinghies, catamarans, and yachts, as well as water-skiing and windsurfing. If your skills are up to par, you can take a vessel out or participate in one of the resort's yacht or dinghy regattas. Waters are most challenging during the winter months, but summer usually brings milder trade winds and conditions better suited to beginners.

Sunsail is the perfect resort for water-lovers!

CURTAIN BLUFF HOTEL
Morris Bay
Antigua, West Indies
☎ (268) 462-8400; fax (268) 462-8409
Reservations: ☎ (888) 289 9898
www.curtainbluff.com
Deluxe

Curtain Bluff is exclusive and elegant.

This exclusive hotel, home of one of the Caribbean's best wine cellars, is located on a private peninsula with two beaches. The all-inclusive property includes all meals, drinks, afternoon tea, watersports, tennis, golf, and even mail service so you can send those postcards home.

ANTIGUA VILLAGE
Dickenson Bay
St. John's, Antigua, West Indies
☎ (268) 462-2930

Antigua

Reservations: ☎ (800) 447-7462
Moderate

Located at the edge of Dickenson Bay, this village
is composed of Mediterranean-style villas on a
one-mile stretch of sand. Studio, one- , and two-
bedroom apartments are available and include either a patio or balcony.

HAWKSBILL RESORT
St. John's, Antigua, West Indies
☎ (268) 462-0301; fax (268) 462-1515
Reservations: ☎ (800) 223-6510
www.hawksbill.com
Moderate-Expensive

Hawksbill is the location of Antigua's only nude beach.

Located just a few minutes from St. John's, this
quiet resort is our favorite kind: quiet, restful,
and located on not one but four superb beaches.
With a primarily British contingency, the resort
is somewhat reserved but is just a few minutes
from the action of St. John's. The 37-acre property
includes cottages and low-profile buildings that
house 113 units. Nudists can wander over to the
fourth beach to seek a total tan at the only nude
beach in Antigua.

GALLEON BEACH CLUB
English Harbour, 30 minutes from St. John's
St. John's, Antigua, West Indies
☎ (268) 460-1024; fax (268) 460-1450
Reservations: ☎ (800) 223-9815
www.galleonbeach.com
Moderate-Expensive

Located in Antigua's National Park on the island's southern tip, this hotel offers one- and two-
bedroom cottages and suites with fully equipped

kitchens, living rooms, and large sundecks all overlooking the beaches at Freeman's Bay and English Harbour. Complimentary amenities include daily maid service, fresh flowers, ferry service to the dockyard, watersports, tennis, and beach chairs. A restaurant and bar are on the premises.

Villas

Several rental agencies in Antigua and Barbuda offer visitors beautiful and secluded villas. Some of these companies are:

CARIBREP
St. John's, ☎ (268) 463-2070
www.caribrepvillas.com

Caribrep has been in business for 15 years and has offices in Antigua and New York. It offers many villas and cottages in Antigua and Barbuda. For a description of all properties and rate information, visit its website.

ANTIGUA VILLAS
☎ (268) 463-7101
www.antiguavillas.com

Antigua Villas offers fully equipped, fully furnished villas with scenic surroundings. There are several sizes and styles of villas.

TROPICAL RESORT
☎ (718) 657-5814
www.tropicalresort.com/antigua.htm

Antigua

This villa rental company has several locations in Antigua and Barbuda, with rates ranging from Moderate to Deluxe.

Small Hotels

THE ADMIRAL INN
Nelson's Dockyard English Harbour
St. John's, Antigua, West Indies
☎ (268) 460-1027; fax (268) 460-1534
Inexpensive-Moderate

Located right in Nelson's Dockyard, this 17th-century building now offers 14 guest rooms (each with twin beds). Each is decorated with antiques, wrought-iron chandeliers, and hand-hewn beams; some rooms feature air conditioning. The inn hosts the awards ceremonies for April's Sailing Week, so book very early for that peak time.

Best Places to Eat

The Alive Price Scale

Expensive. . . . . US $40+ per person
Moderate . . . . $25-$40
Inexpensive . . . . Under $25

Visa, Mastercard, American Express and Diners Club are commonly accepted; Discover is accepted at some establishments.

> ### ⑨ *AUTHOR'S TIP*
>
> Some restaurants add a 15% gratuity to the bill, so make sure you don't inadvertently tip twice.

Island Specialties

At the resort restaurants, you'll find familiar dishes on the menu as well as a few island specialties, such as **christophine** (a type of squash), **pepperpot** (a spicy stew), **afungi** (a pudding of cornmeal and okra), and **ducana** (a pudding made from grated sweet potato and coconut, sugar and spices, boiled in a banana leaf). Save a little room to finish off your meal with a taste of the sweet **Antigua black pineapple**. The most popular beer on the island is **Wadadli**, made locally.

Caribbean Cuisine

LOOKOUT RESTAURANT
Shirley Heights, All Saints, Antigua
☎ (268) 460-1785
Inexpensive-Moderate

With views of Nelson's Dockyard, this restaurant serves up local specialties: spiny lobster soup, codfish balls, Antiguan pineapple, and grilled lobster with lime butter. Steel bands entertain on Sunday afternoons.

Antigua

HEMINGWAYS' VERANDA BAR AND RESTAURANT

St. Mary's Street, St. John's, Antigua
☎ (268) 462-2763
Moderate

Located near Heritage Quay, this informal, second-story restaurant is located in a West Indian-styled building constructed in the early 1800s. Start with a Hemingways' fruit punch or pineapple daiquiri then move on to an entrée of Caribbean seafood or steak.

Continental Cuisine

ADMIRAL'S INN

Nelson's Dockyard
St. John's, Antigua
☎ (268) 460-1027
Inexpensive-Moderate

This inn is also home to a very popular eatery with outdoor dining near the yachts that come to this dockyard from around the Caribbean. Along with great people-watching, the restaurant also offers breakfast, lunch, and dinner. Save time before dinner for a stop by the lounge area, which is filled with yacht club flags.

CALYPSO CAFE

Redcliffe Street, St. John's, Antigua
☎ (268) 462-1965
Inexpensive

This café offers a variety of local dishes as well as Continental cuisine in a garden setting.

REDCLIFFE TAVERN
Redcliffe Quay, St. John's, Antigua
☎ (268) 461-4557
Inexpensive-Moderate

Just steps from the shopping district of St. John's, this restaurant is housed in a red-brick former warehouse that dates back to the 19th century.

Redcliffe selections: quiche, sirloin steak, smoked salmon, seafood.

VIENNA INN
Fort Road, Hodges Bay
St. John's, Antigua
☎ (268) 462-1442
Inexpensive-Moderate

Austrian food in Antigua? Why not? When you're ready for a break from island fare, stop by this eatery for Swiss schnitzel, veal filled with ham and cheese and topped with egg, Wiener schnitzel, or veal schnitzel.

French Cuisine

CHEZ PASCAL
Galley Bay Hill, St. John's, Antigua
☎ (268) 462-3232
Expensive

Dine in the dining room or the garden at this fine restaurant located at Cross and Tanner streets. This elegant eatery has been offering fine cuisine since 1989.

Antigua

LE BISTRO
Hodges Bay, St. John's, Antigua
☎ (268) 462-3881
Moderate-Expensive

The island's first French restaurant, this eatery is known for its haute cuisine and includes local dishes such as medallions of fresh local lobster in basil, white wine, and brandy sauce. With open windows and plenty of fresh sea breezes, this is a favorite spot with romancers.

Seafood Restaurants

COCONUT GROVE BEACH RESTAURANT
Dickenson Bay Road, 15 minutes from St. John's
☎ (268) 462-1538
Inexpensive-Moderate

Located at the water's edge, this restaurant specializes in fresh lobster and local seafood. It's popular with both tourists and residents. Open for breakfast, lunch, and dinner daily.

Sunup to Sundown

Beaches

Antigua's beaches – tourism folks like to say there are 365 of them, one for every day of the year – are one of its strongest assets. All beaches are open to the public. Here are some top choices for a good beach walk, a day of sunning, or just a little beachcombing; see map for lcoations.

- **Dickenson Bay** and **Runaway Bay**. On the island's northwest side, these resort beaches are developed and offer plenty of fun. About 2½ miles north of St. John's.

- **Fort James**. This northwest beach is very popular with locals. It's 1½ miles northwest of St. John's.

- **Galley Bay**. Located on the northwest bay, this beach attracts surfers during the winter months when wave action is at a peak. Five miles west of St. John's.

- **Half Moon Bay**. Situated on the southeast corner of the island, this beach is a national park. Twenty miles southeast of St. John's.

- **Hawksbill Resort**. There are four beaches at this resort on the northwest side, the last of which is clothing-optional. Five miles west of St. John's.

- **Long Bay**. Located on the east side of the island, this beach boasts calm waters protected by a reef and is a good choice for snorkelers and families. Fifteen miles east of St. John's.

- **Rendezvous Bay**. This southern coast beach is a quiet spot for those seeking solitude. Twenty miles south-southeast of St. John's.

Antigua

Scuba Diving

Antigua has a good variety of scuba sites: shallow reefs, deep coral canyons, caves, and wrecks.

Good visibility (from 50 to over 100 feet) and little or no current at most sites provides for good diving conditions. The water temperature averages about 80°.

Some of Antigua's top scuba sites include:

- ◎ **Sunken Rock.** Advanced divers appreciate this deep site, with a maximum depth of over 120 feet. The dive begins at 40 feet in a coral canyon that descends a sandy ledge. Divers then proceed down a drop-off to the bottom of the ocean. Barracuda, amberjack, and rays are usually found here.

- ◎ **The Chimney.** Located southwest of Antigua, this dive features a small cave at a depth of 60 feet, with sponge-filled gullies descending to 80 feet. Look for large parrot fish, lobsters, eels, and nurse sharks in the vicinity.

- ◎ **Red Rock.** This 70-foot dive is known for its expansive coral reef dotted with barrel sponges and sea fans. Located just west of Falmouth Harbour.

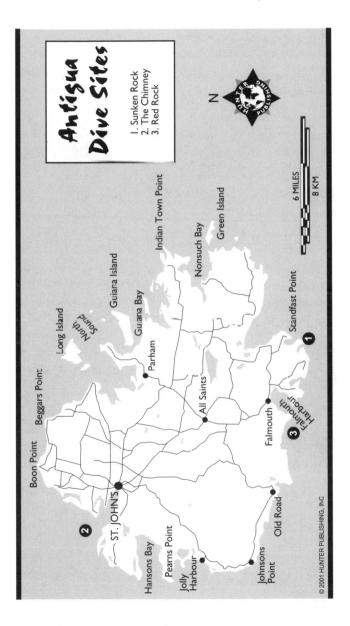

Antigua

© 2001 HUNTER PUBLISHING, INC

Dive Operators

Certification is required and these operators offer lessons for full certification or resort courses.

Aquanaut Diving Centers has locations at: Galleon Beach Club, ☎ (268) 460-1024; Royal Antiguan Resort, ☎ (268) 462-3733; and St. James Club, ☎ (268) 460-5000.

You might also try one of the following:

> **Dive Antigua**
> Rex Halcyon Cove
> ☎ (268) 462-0256
>
> **Dive Runaway**
> Runaway Beach Club
> ☎ (268) 463-2005
>
> **Jolly Dive**
> Jolly Beach Hotel
> ☎ (268) 462-7245
>
> **Long Bay Dive Club**
> Long Bay Hotel
> ☎ (268) 463-2005

Snorkel Excursions

There's good snorkeling at many sites around Antigua. We enjoyed snorkeling off **Hawksbill**. **Cades Reef** is another favorite.

If you'd like to experience a wreck dive without donning the gear, try snorkeling over the wreck of **_The Andes._** This merchant ship sank in 1905 and can be seen in less than 30 feet of water. It is located in Deep Bay, about five miles west of St. John's.

Sailing

Sailing is serious business on this island; many call Antigua the sailing capital of the Caribbean. The annual **Sailing Week** (see *Holidays*, page 50) attracts boaters from around the globe to English Harbour Town and is considered one of the world's top regattas. It's certainly the largest in the Caribbean, and draws some of the globe's fastest yachts and top crews.

Sailing Week isn't all work and no play, however. The week is filled with parties, barbecues, road races, and ends with a grand finale, **Lord Nelson's Ball**.

Whenever you visit, you can enjoy a leisure cruise, one that might include lunch, sightseeing, snorkeling, and entertainment.

Some fun cruises include:

Jolly Roger Pirate Cruise
☎ (268) 462-2064
Antigua's largest sailing ship, this two-masted schooner has daily cruises.

Wadadli Cats (catamaran)
☎ (268) 462-2980

Kokomo Cats (catamaran)
☎ (268) 462-7245

Antigua

Windsurfing

Constant northeast trade winds make this a good windsurfing destination. Beginners learn on the west coast, with its more protected waters, while the east coast challenges surfers of any level. The center of the windsurfing action is **Dickenson Bay**. Here the annual **Windsurfing Antigua** is scheduled (see page 50 for details).

Look for rentals from **Wadadli Watersports Center** at Buccaneer Cove and **Unlimited Hydro Sports** at Dickenson Bay and Jolly Beach. Windsurfing lessons are offered at several hotels including **Jolly Beach's Windsurfing Sailing School** (considered one of the top schools in the world).

Weekly equipment rentals run about US $200. Lessons start at US $25.

Fishing

Grouper, snapper, and other game fish are sought on deep-sea charters. These waters are the site of two annual tournaments: the Sports Fishing Tournament and the Winter Fishing Tournament.

The **Sports Fishing Tournament** offers over US $50,000 in prizes. The angler who breaks the blue marlin record (771.25 pounds, set in 1994) wins $10,000. Cash prizes also go to the record-breaking catches of white marlin, sailfish, king-fish, wahoo, dolphin and tuna.

The tournament donates part of its proceeds to a local cause or charity. Last year's event assisted the island of Montserrat, a member of the Leeward Islands that has been troubled by constant volcanic threat activity.

About 70 boats participated in the 1999 event. Special fields include the largest fish caught by a female angler, the largest caught by a participant aged 16 and younger, and the most fish tagged and released by any one boat.

The entry fee is US \$50 per angler for members, \$70 for non-members, and includes two days of fishing and admission and dinner at the presentation party. For information and an entry form for this June event, ☎ (268) 462-1961.

Check with your hotel activity desk for charter recommendations, or contact one of these companies directly:

Legend
☎ (268) 462-0256
A 35-foot Hatteras Sportfishing boat based at Rex Halcyon Cove.

Lobster King
☎ (268) 462-4364
A 38-foot Bertram available for full- and half-day charters from Jolly Harbour.

Overdraft
☎ (268) 462-0649
A 40-foot fiberglass fishing boat.

Antigua

Golf

The most challenging course is at **Cedar Valley Golf Club**, ☎ (268) 462-5635. This 18-hole, par-70 course includes views of the north coast and is located three miles from St. John's. It was designed by the late Ralph Aldridge to fit the island's contour. In mid-March, the **Antigua Open** is played here by some of the Caribbean's top golfers. A nine-hole course is available at **Half Moon Bay Hotel**, ☎ (268) 460-4300.

Tennis

Tennis is a top sport in Antigua with good courts found at hotels and private tennis clubs. May's **Antigua Tennis Week** is hosted at the **Curtain Bluff Hotel**, ☎ (268) 462-8400, a property that includes four championship courts, two lit for night play, and a full-time pro. **St. James Club**, ☎ (268) 460-5000, has seven lighted all-weather tennis courts with a center court for tournaments. **Half Moon Bay Hotel**, ☎ (268) 460-4300, hosts three professional tennis tournaments: the Men's International Tennis Championship in January; Women's International Tennis Week in April, and a Mixed Doubles Tennis Tournament in October. The property has five all-weather Laykold tennis courts, a teaching pro, and pro shop.

Temo Sports, ☎ (268) 460-1781, is a tennis and squash complex with synthetic grass tennis courts lit for night play. Round-robin tennis tournaments are often scheduled, and vacationers are welcome to join.

Unique Tours

Caribbean Helicopters offers visitors a truly unique view at Antigua. A 15-minute tour looks at half of the island, and a 30-minute tour covers the whole island. To book a flight or for more information, contact Caribbean Helicopters at ☎ (268) 460-5900.

Nature Tours

Eco Sea Tours, ☎ (268) 463-0275, offers several tours that show visitors the natural beauty of the islands. Raft tours to Barbuda allow visitors to snorkel and observe the underwater life, and also afford a good view of The Frigate Bird Sanctuary. Other tours show you the sights of Antigua. Visit their website, www.ecoseatours.com for tour and rate information.

Island Sightseeing

Walking Tour, St. John's

The capital of Antigua is home to about 35,000 residents and is the center of both business and tourist activity. Take a stroll around this historic

city for a look at **St. John's Cathedral**, perched on a hilltop overlooking the town. It was first constructed in 1682 and later replaced in 1789. It was rebuilt and reconsecrated in the 19th century after a devastating earthquake and includes two Baroque-style towers. Also take a walk by **Government House**, the official residence of the Governor General of Antigua, and a good example of 17th-century colonial architecture.

PUBLIC MARKET
Market Street

This semi open-air market is the place to go for local color and culture. Vendors sell their produce and locals stock up on fresh vegetables, spices, and fish in this genuine Caribbean establishment. Open Friday and Saturday.

HERITAGE QUAY

This shopping complex is just steps from the cruise-ship pier off High Street and is home to duty-free shops.

REDCLIFFE QUAY

Also a popular shopping district for vacationers, this restored arsenal houses shops as well as restaurants. The Quay also offers visitors a glance back into the history of Antigua. Before the abolition of slavery on Antigua in 1834, the area was used as a holding place for slaves.

St. James

MUSEUM OF ANTIGUA AND BARBUDA

Located in the **Old Courthouse**, this museum includes exhibits of artifacts tracing the history of the islands from prehistoric times through independence. It offers displays on native artifacts, tools, island foliage, as well as on the history of the island.

English Harbor Area

NELSON'S DOCKYARD NATIONAL PARK
English Harbour

Built in 1784, this was the headquarters of Admiral Horatio Nelson, the commander of the Leeward Islands fleet. This site is a "must-see" on Antigua, even if you're not a maritime-history buff. Make time to visit the **Dow's Hill Interpretation Centre** at the park, which has exhibits on history, culture, and nature. The "Reflections of the Sun" multimedia presentation traces the history of Antigua and Barbuda from prehistoric times to the present.

COPPER AND LUMBER STORE
English Harbour

The Copper and Lumber Store Hotel was once a bustling center of marine activity near the docks. The bottom story served as a supply store and the upper floors were used as quarters for sailors whose ships were being hauled in for repairs. Today those quarters are elegant rooms of a Geor-

Antigua

gian hotel and filled with period furnishings. Two other buildings, the old **Capstan House** and the **Cordage and Canvas Store**, have been restored for additional hotel space by the Copper and Lumber owners. Call for opening times, ☎ 268-460-1058.

ADMIRAL'S HOUSE
English Harbour

The museum (just look for the bust of Nelson framed in the doorway) is an original structure and is filled with mementos of England's most famous naval commander. Open 8:30-4:30; ☎ 268-460-8181.

CLARENCE HOUSE
English Harbour

This was once the home of Prince William Henry, Duke of Clarence, who later became King William IV. The Georgian stone residence overlooks the dockyard and is now home to the Governor General. When he is not in residence, the home is open to the public with tours on the house's origins and history. Open 8-4 daily; ☎ 268-462-0083.

SHIRLEY HEIGHTS
Nelson's Dockyard National Park

Located north of English Harbour, these ruins were named for General Thomas Shirley, former governor of the Leeward Islands. The fortress includes extensive fortifications, barracks, and powder magazines that serve as good places to enjoy the view. On Sunday afternoons, Shirley Heights is a gathering spot where vacationers can come to enjoy local reggae and steel bands and traditional barbecue while watching the sun set over the dockyard. Walkers and hikers can reach Shirley Heights on the **Lookout Trail**. This nature walk ascends from the harbor through a thicket of trees.

FORT BERKELEY
Nelson's Dockyard National Park

About a 10-minute walk from the dockyard, these ruins were once a small outpost with eight cannons.

Out-of-Town Sights

BETTY'S HOPE ESTATE
Near Pares Village, about 10 miles southeast of St. John's

This plantation introduced large-scale sugar cultivation and innovative methods of processing sugar to the island. Founded in the 1650s by Governor Keynell and granted to Christopher Codrington in 1688, the Codrington family had interest in Betty's Hope for more than 250 years until 1920. Both Christopher Codrington and his son served as the Governor General of the Leeward Islands. Today, two windmill towers remain standing along with walls and arches of the boiling house. A recently completed conservation project has refurbished this site.

Take Main Road to Willikies and Long Bay then turn south onto the dirt road that leads to Betty's Hope.

Antigua

HARMONY HALL
Brown's Bay, near Freetown, about 20 miles southeast of St. John's

One of the Caribbean's most noted art galleries, Harmony Hall features regularly scheduled exhibits and shows. The complex includes a great house, now home to a gift shop and galleries, and a sugar mill, first restored in 1843, which offers a 360° lookout over the waters of Nonsuch Bay. These buildings were formerly part of the Montpellier Sugar Estate and today the complex also includes two guest cottages on six acres of land. Lunch is served daily at the Mill Bar and Restaurant (dinner on Thursday, Friday, and Saturday evenings) with local fare. For more information, ☎ (268) 460-4120.

INDIAN TOWN NATIONAL PARK
East of St. John's about 15 miles on Main Road, near Willikies on Nonsuch Bay

The island's eastern end is home to Indian Town Point, which may have been an old Arawak campsite. Look for the **Devil's Bridge**, a limestone arch on the seashore. Blowholes often form when the waves are at a peak. The park is worth a stop. Be sure to bring your camera.

Shop Till You Drop

In Antigua, a shopper's only dilemma is where to start. The selection is one of the best in the entire region and most stores are located within walking distance of each other. Top purchases include: perfume, cosmetics, fine watches, leather goods, linens, sweaters and china.

The primary shopping area on the island is in **St. John's**, near the cruise-ship terminal. It's worth a two- or three-hour excursion to have a look at the goods offered in the small boutiques.

Along the waterfront you'll find the most tourist-oriented shopping, with duty-free wares such as fine jewelry, perfumes, and liquor. Look for Gucci, Colombian Emeralds, Little Switzerland, and other fine shops at **Heritage Quay**. Besides these pricey gift items, you'll also find a good selection of tropical prints and batik fabric sportswear (made on the island) sold in this area. Caribelle Batik has an excellent selection of shirts, skirts, and shorts in tropical colors.

Nearby, **Redcliffe Quay** is a more scenic place to shop and have a drink or some lunch. You won't see the duty-free shops of Heritage Quay here, but you will find plenty of cool shade, brick courtyards, and restored buildings where you can shop for Caribbean items or enjoy a cold beer in a charming atmosphere.

If you'd like to get away from the tourist center, take a walk up to **Market Street** for shops aimed at the local residents, including many fabric stores offering beautiful tropical prints.

Outside of St. John's, head to **Harmony Hall** in **Brown's Bay Mill**. This art gallery, ☎ 268-460-4120, which originated in Jamaica, features work by many Caribbean artists. Original works as well as prints and posters are for sale, accompanied by crafts, books, and seasonings that capture the spice of the island.

Real Bargains?

You won't find equal savings on all goods so do some research in your hometown stores to see if the savings are real.

In Antigua, baubles from around the world will tempt you. Just how good are the bargains? You'll want to do some research before you leave home to determine how real the discounts are but expect to see the biggest savings on high-ticket items such as fine jewelry and watches.

Price Comparisons

Here are some sample prices (in US dollars) we saw during a recent shopping trip:

Jewelry: ½-carat diamond drop, $1,100; ¾-carat diamond drop, $1,900; 14k gold earrings with small porpoises, $100; 14k tanzanite and diamond ring, $4,400; 18k gold band with ½-carat small diamonds, $600; Carrera y Carrera Romantic Collection, Romeo and Jullietta ring, $850.

Men's Watches: Breitling 18k gold and stainless steel, $2,900; Breitling 18k gold Chronomat with mother of pearl dial, $16,000; Ebel "Modulor" stainless steel chronograph, $2,800; Ebel "Topwave" 18k gold and stainless steel, $940; Gucci "7700" stainless steel, $675; Gucci "9045" stainless steel, $470; Longines "Dolce Vita" stainless steel chronograph, $950; Omega "MarsWatch" titanium, $2,400; Omega "Seamaster" stainless steel, $1,400; Rado "Ceramica," $1,350; Raymond Weil "Parsifal" 18k gold and stainless steel, $1,400; Raymond Weil "Tango" stainless steel, $475; Raymond Weil "W1" stainless steel, $600; Swiss Army "Officer" stainless steel, $233; Swiss Army "Renegade" with compass, $75; Tag Heuer "6000" stainless steel chronometer, $1,850; Tag Heuer "Kirium" stainless steel chronograph, $1,500; Tissot "Ballade" 18k gold plated, $320; Tissot titanium, $360; Yves Saint Laurent "EXP 101" Chronograph, $145; Yves Saint Laurent "SNL 650" stainless steel chronograph, $750.

Ladies Watches: Breitling "Callistino" 18k gold and stainless steel, $1,900; Breitling "J-Class" 18k gold and stainless steel $2,800; Ebel sport 18k and stainless steel with diamond dial, $3,700; Gucci "2305" 18k gold, $600; Gucci "6700" stainless steel, $500; Longines "La Grand Clasique," $680; Rado "Integral Jubile" with diamond dial, $1,400; Rayond Weil "Chorus" 18k gold plated, $550; Swiss Army "Officer," $300; Tag Heuer "2000 Evolution" $800; Tag Heuer "Kirium" stainless steel, $1,200; Yves Saint Laurent 18k gold bangle watch, $150; Yves Saint Laurent 18k gold-plated mother of pearl diamond dial, $185.

Collectibles: Hummel figurine "Bahamas News," $240; Lalique Baccantes vase, $2,700; Lenox five-place-setting dinner plates, "Autumn" design, $48; Lladró Angel with Flute, $80; Lladró Mirage, $220; Royal Doulton vase, $35;

Swarovski silver crystal miniature crab, $50; Waterford Lismore champagne flute, $44.

Leather Goods: Bally black belt with silver buckle (men's), $100; Bally briefcase with silver trim, $660; Bally wallet, $120; Salvatore Ferragamo Gancini bag, $380; Salvatore Ferragamo wallet, $180; Versace wallet, $160.

Perfumes & Fragrances: Allure for women (1.7 oz.), $44; Blue Jeans for men (2.5 oz.), $30; Champs Elysses Spray (3.4 oz.), $39.50; CK One (200 ml.), $40; Elizabeth Arden Fifth Avenue (125 ml. spray), $43; Eternity for Men (100 ml spray), $36; Gianni Versace for women (1.6 oz.), $40; Hugo Spray for men (5.1 oz.), $49; Moschino Uomo (2.5 oz.), $38.50; Organza for women (1.7 oz.), $44.50; Pleasures for men (1.7 oz.), $25; Poeme for women (1.7 oz.), $44.50; Tresor for women (1.7 oz.), $44.50.

Can I Mail This Home?

If you've shopped till you dropped and loaded up on presents for the folks back home, you might consider mailing some packages instead of hauling them back through the airports and customs. Here are the rules that govern mailings:

For the US:

> ☺ You can mail home any number of gifts duty free as long as any one recipient doesn't receive gifts totaling more than US $100 in a day.

- You can't mail home gifts of tobacco or liquor.

- You must mark purchases "unsolicited gift" and write this on the outside of the package.

- You cannot send a "gift" to yourself; you'll have to pay duties on these. You can send a package to yourself if the value isn't over $200.

For Canada:

- You can send a gift to Canada duty free if it is worth C $40 or less.

- You cannot mail home gifts of tobacco, liquor, or advertising matter.

For the UK

- You can mail home gifts if you're sending them to a personal friend (as opposed to a business).

- You can send home duty-free gifts if they're not for commercial trade.

- Gifts can't exceed £145.

Fine Jewelry

THE GOLDSMITTY
Historic Redcliffe Quay, St. John's
☎ (268) 462-4601

This shop is full of imperial topaz, tanzanite, black opal jewelry and more, created by famous designer Hans Smit.

Antiques & Antique Jewelry

J & D'S ANTIQUES AND COLLECTIBLES
Upper Long Street, St. John's
☎ (268) 562-0023

Buyers at J & D's can catch many rare finds, from American antiques to West Indian collectibles.

Books

ISLAND NEWSSTAND
Lower High Street, St. John's
☎ (268) 462-2457

Customers can find fiction, newspapers, cards, and postcards at this local mart.

Cameras, Hi-Fi & Audio Equipment

RADIO SHACK
Woods Centre Shopping Mall
☎ (268) 480-2350

Electronics of all kinds can be found at this big-name chain.

Grog & Spirits

MANUEL DIAS LIQUOR STORE
Long and Market Streets, St. John's
☎ (268) 462-0490

Duty-free prices on dozens of wines and liquors.

QUIN FARARA'S LIQUOR STORE
Long Street, St. John's
☎ (268) 462-0463

Wines imported from Italy, California, France, and other well-known regions.

Fashion Boutiques

A THOUSAND FLOWERS
Historic Redcliffe Quay, St. John's
☎ (268) 462-4264

This boutique offers everything from beachwear to fine silks. It also has a wide selection of accessories.

DALILA
Historic Redcliffe Quay, St. John's
☎ (268) 462-3625

Dalila offers shoppers genuine Caribbean wear. Clothes, bags, and jewelry give you the look of the island.

Gifts & Souvenirs

JACARANDA
Historic Redcliffe Quay, St. John's
☎ (268) 462-1888

Clothing, spices, art, and more are available here for customers to take home for mementos.

THE BEST SHOP IN ANTIGUA
Redcliffe Street, St. John's
☎ (268) 462-9758

One of the best places on the island to buy gifts is this shop. With such a wide range of items, you'll have no problem finding the perfect souvenir.

Art Galleries

HARMONY HALL
Brown's Bay, St. John's
☎ (268) 460-4120

A restored 18th-century sugar mill, Harmony Hall displays and sells many local artists' paintings and crafts.

ISLAND ARTS
Heritage Quay, St. John's
☎ (268) 462-2782

Owner Nick Maley sells his art here, as well as work by other Caribbean artists.

After Dark

Bars

ABRACADABRA BAR AND RESTAURANT
English Harbour, Antigua
☎ (268) 460-1732

This local hot-spot has it all: dancing, sports, piano bar, live music; a great place to spend an evening.

BIG BANANA

Historic Redcliffe Quay, St. John's
☎ (268) 480-6985

Live music twice a week and a great selection of
CDs for the other five nights, along with great
food.

COCONUT GROVE BEACH RESTAURANT

Dickenson Bay, Antigua
☎ (268) 462-1538

This beachside bar has a great menu and live music on the weekends.

Be sure to stop by Millers on Sunday for Caribbean Night.

MILLERS BY THE SEA

Fort James, St. John's
☎ (268) 462-9414

Each night of the week offers a different style of
live music.

O'GRADY'S PUB

Redcliffe Street, St. John's
☎ (268) 462-5392

A local favorite, the pub combines its impressive
menu with live music on Wednesday nights.

Casinos

JOE MIKE'S DOWNTOWN HOTEL PLAZA

Nevis Street & Corn Alley, St. John's
Open 6 pm-2 am
☎ (268) 462-1142/3244

Slot machines, table games, and a good restaurant and bar with live music make this a favorite
stop for visitors.

Antigua

KING'S CASINO
Heritage Quay, St. John's
Open 10 am-midnight
☎ (268) 462-1727

Not only does this casino hold the record for the largest casino on the island, but also boasts the largest slot machine in the world. What is a better reason to visit?

ST. JAMES' CLUB CASINO
Momora Bay, St. James'
Open 8 pm-late (depending on the crowd)
☎ (268) 460-5000

Table games and slot machines are available to visitors at this newly renovated casino.

Cinema

DELUXE THEATER LTD.
High Street, St. John's
☎ (268) 462-2188

Antigua A-Z

Consulates

American Consular Section
Bluff House, Pigeon Point, English Harbour
☎ (268) 463-6531

Assists Americans in Antigua and Barbuda, St. Kitts and Nevis, and the British West Indies.

American Express Office
Long and Thames Streets, St. John's
☎ (268) 462-4788

Banks

American Pacific Bank & Trust
Woods Centre
☎ (268) 462-8000

Antigua & Barbuda Development Bank
St. Mary's Street, St. John's
☎ (268) 462-0838

Antigua Commercial Bank
St. Mary's & Thames Streets, St. John's
☎ (268) 462-1217

Barrington Bank
High Street, St. John's
☎ (268) 480-2792

Caribbean Banking Corporation Ltd.
High Street, St. John's
☎ (268) 460-7591

Dentists

Family Dentistry
Cross Street, St. John's
☎ (268) 462-0058

Gentle Dental Services
High Street, St. John's
☎ (268) 462-7276

Williams and Associates Dental Clinic
Long Street, St. John's
☎ (268) 462-1381

Grocery Stores

Convenience Shopping
Glanville
☎ (268) 463-6484

F&F Superette
Potters Village
☎ (268) 462-6625

Mussies Mini Mart
Mussington Piyotts
☎ (268) 462-3629

Food City
Deep Water Harbour, St. John's
☎ (268) 462-4808

Emergency Phone Numbers

General	☎ 911 or 999
Fire	☎ (268) 462-0044
Hospital	☎ (268) 462-0251
Police Emergencies	☎ (268) 462-0125
Disaster Preparedness	☎ (268) 462-4402
Alcoholics Anonymous	☎ (268) 462-3155
Air/Sea Rescue	☎ (268) 465-3062
Ambulance	☎ (268) 462-0251
Domestic Violence	☎ (268) 463-5555

Hospital

Hoberton Hospital
Queen Elizabeth Highway
☎ (268) 462-0251/4

Optical Services

Antigua Vision Center
Independence Drive, St. John's
☎ (268) 461-2020

Eyecare Express
Pelican Mall, Basseterre
☎ (268) 465-2020

Eyeland Optical
Friars Hill Road, St. John's
☎ (268) 462-2020

Pharmacies

The Alpha Pharmacy
Redcliffe Street, St. John's
☎ (268) 462-1112

The City Pharmacy
St. Mary's Street, St. John's
☎ (268) 462-1363

East Side Pharmacy
Cross Street, St. John's
☎ (268) 462-2202

Piper's Pharmacy
All Saints Road, St. John's
☎ (268) 462-0736

Antigua

True Value Pharmacy
All Saints Road, St. John's
☎ (268) 462-0255

Photo Labs

Benjes Department Store
Redcliffe Street, St. John's
☎ (268) 462-0733

Carib Foto
Woods Mall, St. John's
☎ (268) 562-0142

Island Photo
Redcliffe Street, St. John's
☎ (268) 462-1567

Photogenesis
Michael's Avenue, St. John's
☎ (268) 462-1066

Places of Worship

Church Of Christ
Nellie Robinson Street, St. John's
☎ (268) 461-6732

Church Of Jesus Christ Latter Day Saints
Radio Range
☎ (268) 461-2237

Grace Baptist Church
Gambles Terrace
☎ (268) 462-4230

Post Offices

All Saints Road
☎ (268) 460-1087

Nelson's Dockyard
☎ (268) 480-1519

High and Long Street50
s, St. John's
☎ (268) 462-0992

V.C. Bird Airport
☎ (268) 462-3221

Woods Mall
Friars Hill Road
☎ (268) 462-9590

Room Tax

Room tax is 8.5%.

Shoe Repair

Neville's Shoe Repair Shop
25 North Street, St. John's
☎ (268) 462-1987

Spa

Equilibrium Health Spa
Friar's Hill Road, St. John's
☎ (268) 462-7919

Antigua

Telephone Service

For directory assistance, ☎ 411.

Video Rentals

Neighbourhood Video Spot
Warren Road, St. John's
☎ (268) 462-9506

Website

www.antigua-barbuda.org

Barbuda

Mention Barbuda and most people will recognize this tiny isle for one reason: Princess Diana. The seclusion and privacy this island offers has often been sought by the late Diana and other glitterati.

But Barbuda is more than a jetsetter's hideaway, it's also a nature lover's island. Accessible as a day trip from Antigua or as a vacation destination of its own, this small island is much less developed that its larger sister. Outside the lavish resorts, the island belongs to the wildlife, primarily of the feathered variety. It's also noted for its spectacular beaches, long stretches of either pink or white sand that divide the sea from the land.

Along with birders and beach buffs, Barbuda also attracts vacationers looking for quiet fishing, golf, tennis, snorkeling, diving, and beachcombing on its more rugged northeastern Atlantic coast.

Even when Antigua was a vital colony, Barbuda remained unsettled. In 1666, Britain established a colony but it developed slowly. One of the first families was the Codringtons, given a land lease in 1680. The name Codrington remains important in Barbuda today.

Transportation

Taxis

Usually, taxis come to meet the plane at every landing and can take you anywhere you'd like to go. Many taxis are operated by local citizens; hotels can call for a taxi for service anywhere on the island.

Orientation

Barbuda is certainly small enough for you to get a real feel for, even as a day tripper. The only "major" settlement is the village of **Codrington**, located near the center of the island. Codrington, home of the island's 1,400 residents, is also home to the island's airstrip, which has only prop service.

The island is rimmed with excellent, undeveloped beaches. A few properties, such as the K Club, are located directly on the water.

⊚ NOTE

All beaches are public, although non-guests of a waterfront property are not permitted above the high water line.

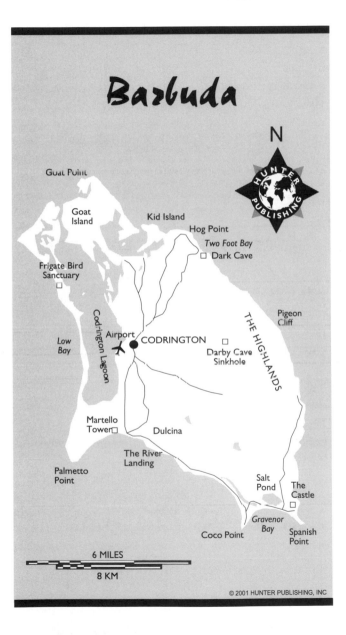

Barbuda

Goat Point

Goat Island

Kid Island

Hog Point

Two Foot Bay
☐ Dark Cave

Frigate Bird
Sanctuary
☐

Pigeon
Cliff

THE HIGHLANDS

Codrington Lagoon

Airport ✈ ● CODRINGTON ☐

Darby Cave
Sinkhole

*Low
Bay*

Martello
Tower ☐

Dulcina

The River
Landing

Palmetto
Point

Salt
Pond

The
Castle
☐

*Gravenor
Bay*

Coco Point

Spanish
Point

N

6 MILES

8 KM

© 2001 HUNTER PUBLISHING, INC

Barbuda

On the west side of the island lies **Codrington Lagoon**, which attracts hundreds of birds. The lagoon is separated from the sea by a narrow stretch of land, home of the **Frigate Bird Sanctuary**.

> ### ★ DID YOU KNOW?
>
> The wingspan of the massive frigate bird can reach eight feet.

Best Places to Stay

Accommodations are few in Barbuda. Room prices vary greatly with type of accommodation, location, and time of year. High season (mid-December through mid-April) brings prices about 40% higher than in summer months.

The Alive! Price Scale

Deluxe	US $300+
Expensive	$201-$300
Moderate	$100-$200
Inexpensive	Under $100

Resort

K CLUB
South of airport 9 miles on Main Road
☎ (268) 460-0300; fax (268) 460-0305
Reservations: ☎ (800) 223-6800

E-mail: k-club@candw.ag
Deluxe

This is one of the Caribbean's most secluded resorts, the spot to which the late Princess Di often went to get away from it all. The resort includes 40 guest rooms on the beach with kitchenettes, gardens, showers, and air conditioning. Rates include all meals. The resort includes a championship nine-hole golf course and two lighted tennis courts. The rates are astronomical, even by high Caribbean standards. If you have to ask, you probably can't afford to stay here. Call for rates.

The K Club is one of the Caribbean's most exclusive properties.

Small Inns

COCO POINT LODGE
Coco Point
Hodges Bay, Barbuda
☎ (212) 986-1416, on-island ☎ (268) 462-3816;
fax (268) 462-5340
Deluxe

On the southern end of Barbuda lies this small resort with 32 rooms, each with a bath and beachfront patio. Small cottages offer kitchenettes.

The resort is tucked on a private, expansive property with plenty of beach to explore. The rates here, although high, are all-inclusive and offer three meals daily, with beverages available anytime. Guests also have a full menu of activities from which to choose, including fishing, tennis and windsurfing.

This resort, which has its own airstrip, is open only from December through May.

Barbuda

PALMETTO BEACH HOTEL
☎ (268) 460-0442, fax (267) 460-0440
Reservations: ☎ (866) BARBUDA
www.palmettohotel.com
Deluxe

Also a pricey property, Palmetto Beach Hotel does offer a lot for the money. Prices range from US $170-250 per person, which includes breakfast, lunch, and dinner, but not drinks. Children under 12 sharing a room with parents stay for free. The resort is closed from September through November, the island's slowest season.

The property has been recently refurbished. It features 24 junior suites and is set on a great stretch of beach (which all rooms overlook). Meals here have a Mediterranean flair, a reflection of the Italian owners. When it's time to work off some of those calories, guests find plenty of options, including scuba diving, snorkeling, excursions to the bird sanctuary, horseback riding, tennis, windsurfing, and more.

REDONDA

If you've been thinking that Barbuda's the most remote spot in the region, think again. The country of Antigua and Barbuda is also home to a third tiny island: Redonda. This uninhabited islet, just one-half square mile, is 35 miles southwest of Antigua. The island's chief inhabitants are feathered ones, including the burrowing owl.

Best Place to Eat

Dining is fairly limited on Barbuda. Many travelers staying in accommodations with kitchen facilities cater for themselves (they have to bring food with them either from home or from Antigua). Another option is to purchase fish fresh from the fishermen who arrive on the docks daily at the Lagoon Wharf. You'll also often find local events and fish-fry festivals on weekends; check with your hotel for these fun events that give a peek into local life.

PALM TREE RESTAURANT
Park Area, Codrington
☎ 268-460-0092
Inexpensive

This casual restaurant serves up traditional cuisine and is especially noted for its seafood dishes. It is a favorite with locals and a great spot to absorb the island scene.

Sunup to Sundown

Much activity on Barbuda is self-guided, although hoteliers and local citizens can help point travelers in the right direction. The island is perfect for vacationers in search of their own fun, whether that means a quiet beach walk, a day of birding, or a lazy swim.

Barbuda

Hiking

Barbuda is well known for its beaches, especially the pink ones on the southwestern shore. The eastern shore beaches face the Atlantic and the waters here are rougher, but these beaches are best for beachcombing.

Walkers will find some good stretches along this windward side of the island. The eastern shore is home to the **Highlands**, steep cliffs that contain many caves, some carved with Amerindian petroglyphs. Sites near **Two Foot Bay**, on the island's northeast side (see map) are favored by hikers. Another favorite, a few miles from the Highlands, is **Darby Cave Sinkhole**, located deep in the bush.

Biking

With its unpaved roads, little traffic, and flat terrain, Barbuda make for a fun bike ride. Check out **Barbuda Bike Tours** (www.barbudabiketours. com), which offers guided bike tours starting at US $25 per day for a few hours of touring. The company also offers bike rentals as well as tent and hammock rentals.

Birding

One of the Caribbean's top birding sites is on tiny Barbuda. The **Frigate Bird Sanctuary**, at the north end of Codrington Lagoon, is accessible only by boat and offers visitors a rare chance to view these imposing birds. Magnificient frigate birds (*Fregata magnificens*) brood their eggs in mangrove bushes along this lagoon. With a wingspan measuring up to a staggering eight feet, the frigate bird or "man o'-war" can fly to 2,000 feet. It is avoided by other birds because it often slams into them in an attempt to get them to disgorge their food, which they quickly gobble up.

The frigate bird is easy to spot, especially the male. During mating season, which runs from September to February, the male inflates a crimson pouch on his throat to try to attract the female. Chicks hatch between December and March and remain in the nest for up to eight months.

Other species often spotted at the sanctuary include pelicans, warblers, snipes, ibis, herons, kingfishers, tropical mockingbirds, oyster catchers, and cormorants.

Nature lovers can also keep an eye out for white-tailed deer, boar, donkeys, and red-footed tortoises as they travel around the island.

Caving

Dark Cave is an underground cavern with deep pools of clear water that extend approximately one mile underground. It's located at Two Foot Bay, north of Codrington. Visitors can climb down into a circular chamber through a hole in the roof

Barbuda

to view faded Arawak drawings on the walls. For directions and a local guide, check with your hotel. Note that on some maps this is called "The Caves."

The **Darby Cave Sinkhole** is another favorite, about 80 feet deep. You'll need to hire a guide (see *Guided Tours*) to take you to this natural sinkhole deep in the bush.

Scuba Diving

Approximately 89 shipwrecks lie off the Barbuda shore, many of which have not yet been explored. It's an excellent territory for scuba divers and snorkelers.

> **◎ AUTHOR'S TIP**
>
> If you're interested in diving off Barbuda, make arrangements at a dive shop on Antigua first. These operators can have your dive equipment sent by air or boat to Barbuda.

Golf

The **K-Club** (see *Best Places to Stay*) has its own nine-hole course. Golf is open for guests only. The cost is US $120 with a golf pro or US $50 without a golf pro. For information, ☎ (268) 460-0300.

Guided Tours

You can arrange for a guided tour of Barbuda in Antigua. **Barbuda Tours/Earls Tours**, located in St. John's, offers a guided look at the island's top sights, including Martello Tower, the Bird Sanctuary, and more. Call ☎ (268) 461-7388 or (268) 462-0742.

Several Barbuda residents also offer guided tours. Call **George Burton** (☎ 268-460 0103) or **Hilroy Thomas** (☎ 268-460 0015), both of whom offer customized excursions to suit your interests.

Island Sightseeing

Barbuda has several attractions. The ruins of **Martello Tower**, a beachside fortress, is one of the last of its kind in the Caribbean. This former lookout now affords some breathtaking views. South of airport on Main Road.

Spanish Point Tower (or The Castle) is another good lookout. Located on the island's southeast side, this tower was originally built to defend the island from the fierce Caribs. Take the Main Road south from the airport.

Barbuda A-Z

Website

www.antigua-barbuda.org.

St. Kitts & Nevis

A Capsule History

The story of St. Kitts and Nevis began long before European discovery. The islands' first settlers were the Carib Indians, a fierce people known for their cannibalism. These first residents called St. Kitts *Liamuiga*, or "fertile land." (Today you'll still hear that name – it graces the island's volcano.) It wasn't until 1493, on his second voyage to the New World, that Christopher Columbus spotted the islands. The larger island he first named San Jorge and then renamed St. Christopher for the patron saint of travelers, a name it retains today (St. Kitts is a nickname given to the isle by the British).

Columbus first named the smaller island San Martin but later renamed it *Nuestro Señora de las Nieves*, Our Lady of the Snows, because of the ever-present cloud that circled Mount Nevis and gave it almost a snow-capped look. Today the cloud still lingers over the mountain peak and hints at a lush rain forest that lies beneath its shadows.

Colonization

All remained quiet on these islands until 1623 when the British arrived to colonize St. Kitts. Just a couple of years later, a French ship, looking for a port after a fight with a Spanish galleon, arrived on the island and the two joined forces to annihilate the Carib Indians. Later the French and English worked together to quell a Spanish attack.

The English set about colonizing nearby islands: Antigua, Barbuda, and Montserrat. The French claimed Martinique and Guadeloupe.

But the peace between the British and French was not to last. Skirmishes began by the mid-1600s. For decades, the British and the French fought over St. Kitts. As a result of the fighting, the English built one of the largest forts in the islands, **Brimstone Hill**. Nicknamed the "Gibraltar of the Caribbean," the fortress guarded the island from a point over 400 feet above sea level. Apparently it didn't protect the shoreline well enough, because in 1782 the French captured the fortress and took over control of the island. The next year the tables turned again, and the losers were loaded onto British ships and sent back to the old country.

In 1690, tiny Nevis was hit by a massive earthquake. A resulting tidal wave washed over the capital city of Jamestown, destroying the city, and sunk part of the island.

The Plantation Era

Throughout the 17th century, a plantation system was in place throughout both islands. Nevis was the center of the slave market for many neighboring islands as it was the headquarters for the Royal African Company from 1600 to 1698. A century later, over 10,000 slaves worked the tobacco and cane fields of the island. Over 50 sugar plantations operated on St. Kitts, using sail-driven windmills to grind the sugarcane.

★ DID YOU KNOW?

Not until 1833 was slavery abolished in all British colonies; today, the first Monday in August is still celebrated as Emancipation Day.

The estate plantation system grew less and less important around the island as technological advances developed. Wind-driven power gave way to steam power. In 1912, the sugar railroad was constructed around the island of St. Kitts, soon making the factories on the individual estates obsolete.

As social changes occurred on the island, so did political ones. In 1871, St. Kitts was placed in a federation with Anguilla and soon Nevis was added. The relationship between the islands was always a tumultuous one, with claims from Anguilla that St. Kitts ignored the much smaller isle in terms of representation and aid.

St. Kitts & Nevis Introduction

Modern Times

The ill feelings between the islands continued to rise in intensity. In 1967, an Anguilla rebellion resulted in independence from St. Kitts. The rebellion caught the attention of the world and the tiny island was given the nickname "The Mouse that Roared."

St. Kitts and Nevis remain a part of the British Commonwealth, and the Queen is represented by a Governor-General on St. Kitts with a Deputy Governor-General stationed on Nevis. On Sept. 19, 1983, Nevis and St. Kitts became an independent state with a Prime Minister and House of Assembly.

Timeline

1493 - First recorded history with sighting by Christopher Columbus.

1607 - Captain John Smith landed in Nevis on his way to colonize Virginia.

1623 - British arrived to colonize St. Kitts.

1625 - French settlers arrived on St. Kitts.

1626 - French and British massacred Indians at Bloody Point.

1628 - English settlers colonize Nevis.

1629 - Spanish attacked the islands.

1642 - Population of Nevis was 10,000.

1664 - French exiled British from St. Kitts.

1689 - England won St. Kitts from France.

1706 - France recaptured St. Kitts.

1690 - Nevis was hit by a massive earthquake.

1782 - French captured Brimstone Hill fortress and ruled the island.

1783 - Treaty of Versailles gave St. Kitts to the British.

1787 - Admiral Horatio Nelson married Nevisian Fanny Nisbet at Montpelier.

1793 - British took over St. Kitts.

1833 - Slavery abolished in all British colonies.

1871 - St. Kitts placed in a federation with Anguilla, and soon Nevis was added.

1929 - Charles Lindberg carried the first recorded inward and outward mails to St. Kitts and Nevis. Two years and four months after his trans-Atlantic crossing, the aviator touched down at Pinney's Beach.

1967 - Anguilla declared independence from St. Kitts.

The Islands Today

St. Kitts is a volcanic island of about 68 square miles. Shaped like a guitar or paddle, the most noticeable feature of the island is **Mount Liamuiga** (until 1983 named Mount Misery – not a good addition to the tourist brochures). The volcano has long been dormant but is not completely extinct.

Only 35 miles square, Nevis is a small link in the Caribbean chain but it packs plenty of beauty into its diminutive size. The circular island rises from the sea to the top of Nevis Peak at 3,232 feet above sea level. Steep mountainsides are dotted with coconut palms that wind their way all the way down to the water's edge.

Only one road circles Mount Nevis and the island, working its way from the capital city of Charlestown to communities such as St. George and Newcastle, passing plantations that lie in ruin and others that have been renovated and now serve as charming bed-and-breakfast properties.

The People

St. Kitts and Nevis boast a total population of about 43,000, with the bulk of those residents found on St. Kitts. About 34,000 people reside on St. Kitts, with 9,000 residents on Nevis.

It's a varied population, although most people trace their ancestry to Africa. Former residents of other countries are also found on the islands.

Environment

Plant Life

The plant life found on both St. Kitts and Nevis is bountiful and beautiful, thanks to frequent rains. Vegetation grows thickest in the rain forest areas of both islands, but you'll see a variety of species anywhere you go, including: **bamboo, wild coffee, seagrape, wild cherries, wild sage, mango, silk cotton tree, screw pine** and **soursop**. The **flamboyant** is the national flower of St. Kitts and Nevis. These trees bloom with brilliant red flowers in the winter months. **Breadfruit** was first brought to the islands by Captain Cook. It is a staple of island diets and used much like a potato.

And if you think you see **pineapples** growing on the islands, you're right. A new variety of high sugar content pineapples has been introduced to St. Kitts and Nevis by agriculturists from the Republic of China. Tainung No. 4 and Kain varieties, which usually grow to about six pounds in China, reach 8½ pounds on these tropical isles. One explanation of the fruit's success is the pure water found on both islands and the fertile soil.

Animals

The best known resident of St. Kitts and Nevis is the **African green (vervet) monkey**, a leftover

St. Kitts & Nevis Introduction

of the French occupation of the island centuries ago. The French had brought the monkeys to the island from Africa as pets but today the animals have thrived in the lush forests of St. Kitts and Nevis, outnumbering the human population two to one. They're both the delight of visitors and the bane of residents, with raids on fruit trees often perpetrated by the wily monkeys.

The monkeys do not have a prehensile tail, so they're often seen on the ground, scampering across a lawn in search of a fallen mango. Social like other monkeys, the green monkeys often travel in groups of 30 or 40. Early mornings and late evenings are the best times for spotting this most common resident of St. Kitts and Nevis. Come out at sunset and sunrise for the best chance to view them.

Be sure to look for mongooses in the underbrush and not in the trees.

Another mammal often spotted is the **mongoose**. An import brought to the island from Jamaica, the mongoose was introduced to much of the Caribbean from India to control snakes in the sugar cane fields. Soon a problem in this extermination plan was revealed: once the snakes were eaten, the rat population soared. Unfortunately, mongooses and rats don't keep the same schedule; the rats are sleeping while the mongooses are hunting. The mongooses have become somewhat of a pest on the island and the rats, left to prosper without their natural predator, the snake, have flourished.

Far more beautiful residents are the **butterflies** of Nevis, which are often seen on Nevisian postal stamps as well as in the rain forest. The southern daggertail, the red rim, the mimic, the painted lady, the Caribbean buckeye, the flambeau, the tropical checkered skipper, and many others in the *Nymphaelidae, Heliconiidae, Hesperiidae* and *Pieridae* families can be spotted.

Local families use honey for its medicinal properties, mixing it with lime to ease colds and sore throats.

The tropical **honeybees** found on St. Kitts and Nevis are responsible for more than honey – they pollinate the thousands of blooms that make these islands so brilliant. Documented evidence of honeybees (*Apis mellifera*) on Nevis dates back to 1716 and it has long been a tradition for men to harvest the wild nests with a cutlass or machete.

Since the 1980s, beekeepers in Nevis have managed the bees in movable frame hives, yielding 150 to 200 pounds of honey per hive every year. The bees are valued for their sweet product and for their role in pollinating sea grapes, coconuts, mangroves, mangoes, sweet and sour oranges, genips, and other local plants. The island has no Africanized honey bees and are protected from bee diseases found elsewhere because of the island's geographic isolation.

St. Kitts & Nevis Introduction

Birds

St. Kitts and Nevis is a bird-lover's paradise. The lush foliage is the perfect place for tropical birds to make their home. Some birds that can be found on the islands are:

⊚ **Bananaquit.** This small bird is found throughout the Caribbean and is one of the most distinctive due to its yellow and black coloration. The bananaquit feeds mostly on nectar and is usually found around flowering plants.

◎ **Brown Pelican.** If you're staying at a beachfront hotel, don't be surprised to see a resident brown pelican working the waters just off the coast. We once enjoyed watching a pelican every day of our stay hunting in the clear waters, diving and scooping up fish in his pouched bill, and ignoring the humans on the nearby beach.

◎ **Cattle Egret.** A fairly recent immigrant to the islands, these large white birds are typically seen accompanying cattle in the fields where they feed on insects disturbed by the grazing cattle.

◎ **Greater Antillean Grackle.** This grackle resembles its North American counterpart both in its appearance and its behavior but is somewhat smaller. Glossy black with staring yellow eyes, the grackle is very urbanized, sometimes making a pest of itself around resort dining areas by begging or stealing food from tables.

◎ **Ground Dove.** These small doves are seen everywhere. Look for a slightly pinkish belly. The ground dove tends to gather in small flocks of two to four birds.

◎ **Magnificent Frigate Birds.** With a
wingspan of over seven feet and wings
sharply angled like boomerangs, the
black frigate bird, or man-of-war bird,
is fairly easy to spot. They soar high
over the sea and are aggressive to
other birds – often hitting the red-
footed booby in flight in an attempt to
make it disgorge its food and provide
an easy meal.

◎ **Red-Tailed Hawk.** These large birds
are solitary predators that sometimes
hunt chickens around towns and villages (hence their common name of
chicken hawk), but their main diet consists of rats and birds. Their most distinctive feature is a broad tail that
appears dark red when the sunlight
passes through it.

◎ **Sparrow Hawk.** This small predator
thrives on lizards, insects, and smaller
birds. It can often be seen perched on a
roadside fence or tree branch and can
be identified by its long, straight tail,
brownish back, and hooked bill.

◎ **Zenaida Dove.** This is a large dove,
sometimes reaching 12 inches in
length. It has pinkish brown coloration
with a white streak on its tail feathers
and is frequently seen in pairs, feeding
on the ground. In flight, it emits a
unique whistling, caused by air rush-
ing around its wings.

St. Kitts & Nevis Introduction

Life Undersea

Divers and snorkelers can find many marine treasures in the waters of St. Kitts and Nevis. Often spotted sea-dwellers include lobsters, many kinds of coral, sea fans, sponges, squirrel fish, and other reef fish. Some days, you may be fortunate enough to encounter a sea turtle, stingray or nurse shark.

For many travelers, St. Kitts and Nevis is a destination sought for its underwater attractions, offering excellent scuba diving, snorkeling and deep-sea fishing, along with a variety of marine life. Among the reefs, expect to see brilliant parrotfish, large-eyed squirrelfish, blue tang, stingrays, eagle rays, rock lobster and, if you're lucky, a turtle. Blue marlin, yellowfin tuna, shark and wahoo also reside in the deepest waters.

Look for the following when underwater:

- **Caribbean Spiny Lobster.** These shy marine creatures have no claws like their northern relatives.

- **Common Sea Horse.** These can be seen by divers beneath piers, hiding in soft corals.

- **Conch.** You're probably familiar with this mollusk because of its shell: a beautiful pink curl nearly a foot long that, when blown by those in the know, can become an island bullhorn or a whistle. The shell covers a huge piece of white meat with a rubbery texture, as well as a "foot," the appendage used by the conch to drag itself along the ocean floor in search of food.

⊚ **Eagle Rays.** Most often spotted along undersea walls, they are wary of people. Like the stingrays, eagles are also white-bellied but have patterned topsides, with spots and circles in a white or beige color against a dark gray or brown background. These rays have angular pectoral fins and can reach up to eight feet across.

⊚ **Four-Eyed Butterfly Fish.** This one is easy to spot: just look for a small yellow, gray, white, and black fish who looks like he has four eyes! Two are actually fakes located near the tail, meant to throw off a predator.

⊚ **French Angelfish.** This gray fish has moon-shaped lighter markings. They're not very shy and if you swim up slowly, you can get quite close to these lovely inhabitants.

⊚ **Green Moray Eel.** Often seen under rock crevices during the day, the moray is frightening looking because he constantly opens and closes his mouth. Don't be afraid, though; the eel is just breathing and is generally harmless unless harassed.

- ◎ **Green Sea Turtles.** These turtles have been known to remain underwater for several days without surfacing for air as they seek food. Even in their current protected state, it's not an easy life; only one turtle out of 10,000 eggs laid reaches maturity. The hazards are many: birds, animals, marine life, humans. You name it, it's a threat to these little guys.

- ◎ **Spiny Puffer Fish.** Like his name suggests, the light beige puffer fish (also known as a balloon fish, and one glance tells you why) looks like a little puffed-up ball scooting through the water with its micro-fins; it can inflate itself with water as a defense.

Getting Here

By Air

Most visitors first arrive at St. Kitts' **Robert Llewelyn Bradshaw International Airport** (formerly Golden Rock Airport).

Most jet service is into San Juan, Puerto Rico or nearby St. Martin, Guadeloupe, Antigua, or even the US Virgin Islands. Passengers then transfer to the smaller planes for the short flight to St. Kitts.

From the US, service is available on **American Eagle** and **Continental Express**.

American . . . . ☎ 800-433-7300
www.aa.com

Continental Airlines . . . . ☎ 800-231-0856
www.continental.com

From the UK, jet service is available on **British Airways**, **BWIA**, **Air France**, **Lufthansa**, and **KLM** through gateways in St. Maarten and Puerto Rico.

British Airways . . . . ☎ 800-AIRWAYS
www.britishairways.com

BWIA . . . . ☎ 869-465-3067
www.bwee.com/caribbean

Air France. . . . . ☎ 800-237-2747
www.airfrance.com

Lufthansa . . . . ☎ 800-645-3880
www.lufthansa.com

KLM . . . . ☎ 800-374-7747
www.klm.com

From other Caribbean islands, service is available on **BWIA**, **LIAT**, and **Winair**.

LIAT . . . . ☎ 869-465-2286
www.liat.com

Winair. . . . ☎ 869-465-4069 from St. Kitts
☎ 869-469-5423 on Nevis

St. Kitts & Nevis Introduction

Flight Times to/from St. Kitts

Antigua. . . . . 20 mins

London . . . . 8 hours

Miami . . . . 3 hours

New York. . . . . 4 hours

Puerto Rico . . . . 1 hour

St. Maarten . . . . 20 mins

From St. Kitts, air service to Nevis' small **Newcastle Airport** is served by commuter flights from St. Kitts. **Air St. Kitts/Nevis** and **Nevis Express** whisk visitors from island to island in less than 10 minutes. Carib Aviation offers flights between St. Kitts & Nevis, as well as servicing Anguilla, Antigua, Barbados, Barbuda, the Dominican Republic, Grenada, Guadeloupe, Martinique, Mustique, Puerto Rico, St. Barts, St. Croix, St. Thomas, St. Vincent, Trinidad, Tobago and Union Island.

Air St. Kitts/Nevis . . ☎ 869-469-9241 (Nevis)
☎ 869-465-8571 (St. Kitts)

Nevis Express. . . . . ☎ 869-469-9756
www.nevisexpress.com

Carib Aviation . . . . ☎ 869-465-3055
www.candoo.com/carib

When leaving St. Kitts, there is a departure tax of US $17.

By Cruise Ship

St. Kitts' US $16.25 million cruise ship terminal is located in Basseterre. Visitors arrive just off **Pelican Mall**, a new establishment with 26 shops that feature tropical clothing, locally made goods, and tourist items. Kittitian architecture makes this mall different from the typical mall you might see back home.

Several cruise lines offer port stops in St. Kitts. Schedules change seasonally, but check with these lines:

Cunard . . . . ☎ 800-7-CUNARD
www.cunard.com
First European . . . . ☎ 888-983-8767
www.first-european.com
Princess Cruises . . . . . . ☎ 800-PRINCESS
www.princesscruises.com
Radisson Cruises . . . . ☎ 800-477-7500
www.rssc.com
Royal Caribbean . . . . ☎ 888-313-8883
www.royalcaribbean.com

Inter-Island Travel

To reach Nevis, most travelers take the ferry. Service is available several times daily between the two islands aboard the *Caribe Queen* (☎ 869-465-2521); the journey takes about 45 minutes and costs EC $20 (about US $8) round trip. Departure is from Basseterre, St. Kitts and arrival is in Charlestown, Nevis.

Another option is the **MV *Sea Hustler*** (☎ 869-469-0403), which also makes twice-daily excursions. This service runs every day. Cost is EC $20 or about US $8. Call for ferry schedule.

Inter-island flights are offered by:

Air St. Kitts/Nevis . . . . . . ☎ 869-469-9241
Carib Aviation . . . . ☎ 869-465-3055
LIAT . . . . ☎ 869-465-2286
Nevis Express. . . . . ☎ 869-469-9756

Getting Ready

Sources of Information

Tourism Offices

10 Kensington Court
London W8 5DL
England
☎ 0171-376-0881; Fax 0171-937-6742

Walter Kolb Strabe 9-11
60594 Frankfurt
Germany
☎ 069-96216413; Fax 069-610637

414 E. 75th St., 5th Floor
New York, NY 10021
☎ (800) 582-6208; Fax (212) 7346-6511

365 Bay St.
Suite 806
Toronto, Ontario M5H 2V1 Canada
☎ (416) 368-6707; Fax (416) 368-3934

On-Island Information

St. Kitts

Department of Tourism
Pelican Mall, Bay Road
PO Box 132
Basseterre, St. Kitts
☎ (869) 465-4040 or 465-2620
Fax (869) 465-8794

Hotel and Tourism Association
PO Box 438, Liverpool Row
Basseterre, St. Kitts
☎ (876) 465-5304; Fax (869) 465-7746

Nevis

Nevis Tourism Bureau
Main Street
Charlestown, Nevis, WI
☎ (869) 469-1042; Fax (869) 469-1066

Internet Information

An excellent source of St. Kitts and Nevis information is the web page for the islands, accessible at **www.stkitts-nevis.com**.

Once You Arrive

Credit Cards

Visa, Mastercard, American Express, Diner Club, and Access are commonly accepted; Discover is accepted at some establishments.

Newspapers/Broadcast Media

The islands' newspaper is **The Democrat**, published in Basseterre.

Telephones

St. Kitts and Nevis have excellent telecommunications service thanks to Cable & Wireless Ltd.

You'll find dependable, modern phone and Inter- net service on each of the islands. Cost varies by hotel.

The area code for St. Kitts and Nevis is 869.

Culture & Customs

What to Expect

St. Kitts and Nevis has a West Indian atmosphere and feel. With its long history of British rule, there is a slightly more formal atmosphere in personal relations; people are often introduced as Mr. or Ms. Also, as in most of the Caribbean, it's traditional to greet others with "Good morning" or "Good afternoon" and smile rather than just launching into your question or request.

Language

English is the primary language in St. Kitts and Nevis, and you'll notice it is spoken with a distinct West Indian lilt. Spelling follows British, not American, spellings – such as colour, travellers and centre.

Holidays

Public holidays on both islands are:

New Year's Day . . . . January 1
Carnival Last Lap . . . . January 2
Good Friday . . . . . . variable, as in the US
Easter Monday . . . . variable, as in the US
Labour Day . . . . May 5
Whit Monday . . . . May 19
August Monday . . . . August 5
Culturama Last Lap . . . . August 6
Independence Day . . . . September 19
Christmas Day . . . . December 25
Boxing Day . . . . December 26

These holidays just hint at the special events that take place on both St. Kitts and Nevis. During most holidays and festivals, Nevis comes to life with horse racing. Race days are scheduled during most special events and draw large crowds.

> ### ⊚ AUTHOR'S TIP
>
> For more information on any of the festivals listed below, ☎ (800) 582-6208 or (869) 465-4040. Note that most event dates vary from year to year.

Other festivities throughout the year include the following events.

☼ JANUARY

Horse Races, *Nevis*
Horse racing is sponsored by the Nevis Jockey Club and held at the Indian Castle Race Track. For information, ☎ (869) 469-3477.

Alexander Hamilton Birthday Tea, *Nevis*
Sponsored by the Nevis Island Administration, this tea party is held at the Museum of Nevis History, the birthplace of Alexander Hamilton. Call for exact date; ☎ (800) 582-6208 or (869) 465-4040.

Environmental Awareness Week, *Nevis*
Sponsored by the Nevis Historical and Conservation Society's Environmental Education Committee; ☎ (869) 469-5786 for information.

☼ FEBRUARY

Horse Racing, *Nevis* (see above)

***Tourism Week**, Nevis.*
This eight-day celebration includes cultural expositions, watersports activities, horse racing, culinary contests, and an arts and crafts exhibition.

☀ MARCH

***Special Nelson Memorial Horse Race**, Nevis*
Sponsored by the Nevis Jockey Club and held at the Indian Castle Race Track. ☎ (869) 469-3477.

***House and Garden Tours**, Nevis*
Visit some of Nevis' most historic homes and gardens with these historic tours sponsored by the Nevis Historical and Conservation Society. ☎ (869) 469-5786.

***Nelson/Nesbit Wedding Anniversary Tea**, Nevis*
Held at the Hermitage Plantation Inn, this afternoon tea commemorates the union of Admiral Nelson and Fanny Nesbit.

☀ APRIL

***Easter Monday Horse Races**, Nevis* (see above)

***Kite Flying Competition**, Nevis*
This event is part of the Easter festivities on Nevis and marks the end of a week-long workshop for Nevisian youths on the art of kite-making. Along with the competition, the event includes local food. The competition is held at Cole Hill.

☀ MAY

***Labour Day Horse Races**, Nevis*
Sponsored by the Nevis Jockey Club and held at

the Indian Castle Race Track. This event also includes a Donkey Derby. ☎ (869) 469-3477.

International Museums Day, Nevis

Open houses are held at the Museum of Nevis History at Alexander Hamilton House in Charlestown and the Horatio Nelson Museum at Bellevue. ☎ (800) 582-6208 or (869) 465-4040.

Flower Show, St. Kitts

Discounted rain forest tours are offered at the Flower Show.

Sponsored by the St. Kitts Horticultural Society, this annual show features local gardeners. Admission is EC $10 and includes refreshments.

Leeward Island Cricket Tournament, St. Kitts & Nevis

This event spans May and June and showcases the islands' best cricketers. ☎ (869) 469-5521.

St. Kitts International Triathlon

This grueling event challenges even the best of athletes with a swim, a bike race and a 10K run.

☀ JUNE

Sunfish Regatta, St. Kitts and Nevis

This regional event includes 14-foot Sunfish and sailboards. The race spans the 11 miles from Frigate Bay, St. Kitts to Oualie Beach, Nevis. Food and music make up the festivities.

Guavaberry Caribbean Offshore Regatta, St. Kitts

This competition spans from St. Maarten to Basseterre and includes food and music in the capital city.

Whit Monday Horse Races, *Nevis*
Sponsored by the Nevis Jockey Club and held at the Indian Castle Race Track. ☎ (869) 469-3477.

St. Kitts Music Festival, *St. Kitts*
This annual event draws both local and internationally known artists. Each night of the festival features a different type of music, from reggae and R&B to gospel. End of June.

☼ JULY

Caribbean Cup Race, *St. Kitts and Nevis*
This inter-island race includes both downhill and cross-country competitions. For more information, ☎ (869) 469-9682.

☼ AUGUST

Caribbean Festival of the Arts, *Nevis*
This annual event has features on the history, folklore and culture of the Caribbean. Over 30 countries participate in this showcasing of culinary arts, literary skills, performing arts, film, and more. For more information, ☎ (869) 465-1999.

Horse Racing, *Nevis*
Scheduled for the first Monday in August, this special event commemorates the emancipation of slaves in the British West Indies. Sponsored by the Nevis Jockey Club and held at the Indian Castle Race Track. ☎ (869) 469-3477.

St. Kitts & Nevis Introduction

☀ SEPTEMBER

Independence Week Activities, *St. Kitts and Nevis*
Parades, picnics, dances and cocktail receptions celebrate the islands' independence. These events take place around Independence Day, September 19th.

Independence Day Horse Racing, *Nevis*
Sponsored by the Nevis Jockey Club and held at the Indian Castle Race Track. ☎ (869) 469-3477.

☀ OCTOBER

World Food Day, *Nevis*
Sponsored by the Nevis Historical and Conservation Society. Workshops, exhibitions, food and fairs. Mid-October.

Sports Fishing Tournament, *Nevis*
Headquartered at Oualie Beach Hotel, this event is organized by the Nevis Yacht Club. ☎ (869) 460-9690 for participation information.

☀ NOVEMBER

Tourism Week, *St. Kitts*
A cultural program and watersports festival to celebrate the tourism industry. Mid-November.

Oceanfest, *St. Kitts*
Windsurfers and Sunfish race from Nevis to St. Kitts. Other events include a fishing tournament, beach fête and music. Mid-Movember. ☎ (869) 465-4040.

Thanksgiving Horse Racing, *Nevis* (see above).

☀ DECEMBER

Carnival, *St. Kitts*

From Christmas Eve through January 3rd (pre-Carnival events begin two weeks earlier), the island celebrates with festivals, calypso competitions, parades, street dances and more. This party is a real island spectacular, filled with color and plenty of true Caribbean atmosphere. For information, call the Carnival Office at ☎ (869) 465-4151.

Boxing Day Horse Racing, *Nevis* (see above).

Weddings

Getting married on St. Kitts or Nevis is a simple affair. Either the bride or groom must be a resident of the island for 48 hours prior to the wedding.

Bring along a valid passport or certified birth certificate and, if either party is divorced, present an absolute decree of divorce. If either the bride or groom is widowed, a death certificate is necessary. (If the documents are not in English, a notarized translation must be presented.)

To be married by a Catholic priest, you must bring a letter from your resident priest verifying that you are unmarried and have received necessary instruction. To be married by an Anglican minister, bring a letter from your minister verifying that you are unmarried.

The marriage license fee is EC $200 (or US $80). If you have enjoyed a pre-honeymoon trip on St. Kitts or Nevis for at least 15 days prior to the marriage, the fee goes down to EC $50 or US $20.

The Attractions

These islands are often referred to as "the way the Caribbean used to be." Life is quiet and unspoiled on this two-island nation. Most guests stay in small, locally owned plantation inns that recall the heritage of the Caribbean with period antiques, wide porches to pick up gentle trade winds, and an atmosphere that appeals to travelers who are independent and ready to strike out on their own.

Rugged and tropical, both islands are excellent destinations for hikers, birders, and nature lovers. St. Kitts is the largest of the two, spanning 68 square miles. The island is 23 miles in length and at its widest point is five miles across. For its size, St. Kitts offers varying terrains that range from semi-arid to rain forest, and from flat to nearly impassable. Most of the population lives on St. Kitts with a large percentage in the capital city of **Basseterre** (pronounced bos-TEAR). Throughout the island, modern life and ancient history live side by side as the island is sprinkled with historic sites that date back both to pre-history and to the days of colonization.

St. Kitts

Development has, thankfully, been slow on St. Kitts. Although the island has one all-inclusive property, most hotels are locally owned and managed and provide a genuine Caribbean experience. They're found throughout the island, both at seaside destinations and high in the hills overlooking fields that were formerly part of plantations.

The most noticeable feature of St. Kitts is **Mount Liamuiga** (pronounced Lee-a-mweega), which is usually fringed with a ring of clouds. This dormant volcano, elevation 3,792 feet, is home of the island's tropical rain forest and an excellent destination for eco-travelers. Guided tours take visitors to the far reaches of the forest for a look at this ecosystem.

One area presently being eyed for development is the Southeast Peninsula, a site that, until a few years ago, could be reached only by boat. After the days when the British and the French fought for domination of St. Kitts, the Southeast Peninsula remained impenetrable. Although it was blessed with white sand beaches and palm-fringed coves, this rugged area was inhabited only by a few diehard residents who traveled by boat, and by troupes of green vervet monkeys and shy white-tailed deer.

But then along came the US military. Soon it accomplished what others had tried to do but failed: complete the Dr. Kennedy Simmonds Highway. The US $14 million road now links this final frontier with the rest of the Caribbean island, and the people of St. Kitts are still singing the praises of the troops who made it possible.

Nevis

Just two miles away from St. Kitts lies the tiny island of Nevis (pronounced NEE-vis), covering a total of 36 square miles. Christopher Columbus gave the island its name, inspired by the ever-present cloud that circled the island's **Mount Nevis**, giving it almost a snow-capped look. Today the cloud still lingers over the mountain peak. Home to only 9,000 residents, this country cousin has a charming atmosphere all its own, plus a good share of plantation houses where guests can enjoy a look back at Caribbean history.

Eco-tourism is also a major draw on Nevis. Mount Nevis offers many hikes of varying levels of difficulty. History buffs find numerous sites of interest in the capital city of **Charlestown**.

THE MONKEYS OF NEVIS

Like its sister island, Nevis is home to many vervet monkeys, a reminder of the French occupation of the island centuries ago. When the British took over the island from the French, they didn't mind transporting their enemies back home but they weren't about to let them take along their beloved monkeys, which the French had imported from Africa. The British turned the monkeys loose on the island where they prospered. Today it's estimated that the monkeys of St. Kitts and Nevis outnumber humans two to one. If you get up early or go out after sunset, you'll stand a good chance of spotting one of the primates.

Nevis recognizes the value of its natural beauty and has declared that, by law, no building may be taller than a palm tree.

St. Kitts & Nevis Introduction

The solitude and privacy offered on both islands attract a celebrity clientele. In recent years, the islands have been chosen as a getaway for Oprah Winfrey, Sylvester Stallone, Danny Glover, Robert De Niro and Michael J. Fox among others.

ISLAND FACTS

- ⑤ St. Kitts is 23 miles long and five miles across at its widest point.

- ⑤ Mount Liamuiga is St. Kitts highest elevation, at 3,792 feet.

- ⑤ Nevis covers 36 square miles. St. Kitts covers 68 square miles.

St. Kitts

Transportation

See *Getting Here,* pages 128-9, for information about airlines and cruise ships serving St. Kitts.

Getting Around the Island

Getting around St. Kitts can be accomplished by taxi or rental car, depending on your level of independence and the frequency with which you wish to travel around the island. If you think you'll be journeying down to the Southeast Peninsula and buzzing around the island, it's worth it to rent a car for your stay. Rentals are readily available (see car rental section below).

Taxi rates are set, although these can change. Within Basseterre, you can journey from one point to another for US $3, with the charge of $1 for every 15 minutes waiting period after the first 15 minutes and 50¢ for each additional piece of luggage beyond two. Rates increase between the hours of 11 pm and 6 am.

Car & Jeep Rentals

Driving in St. Kitts and Nevis is on the left.

Driving on St. Kitts requires a temporary driver's license, which costs EC $50. The license is valid for one year and can be obtained from the **Police Traffic Department** located on Cayon Street in Basseterre, ☎ (869) 465-2241.

Rental car rates run about US $55 per day for a mid-size car.

CAR RENTAL COMPANIES	
Caines Rent-A-Car	☎ (869) 465-2366
Choice Car Rental	☎ (869) 465-4422
Delisle Walwyn Car Rental	☎ (869) 465-8449
Holiday Car Rental	☎ (869) 465-6507
Higgins Car Rental	☎ (869) 465-8080
Island Car Rental	☎ (869) 465-3000
Kitts Car Rental	☎ (869) 465-1665
St. Kitts Taxi Association	☎ (869) 465-4253
Sunshine Car Rental	☎ (869) 465-2193
TDC Rentals Ltd.	☎ (869) 465-2991

Driving Tips

Look to the RIGHT before crossing the street!

In true British tradition, traffic keeps to the left side of the road. This can be confusing on your first day behind the wheel so start off a little slower than usual. Most cars are right drive so that will also necessitate a few adjustments. For instance, on our first excursion on the left side of the road we turned on the windshield wipers every time we tried to give a turn signal!

Taxis

In St. Kitts, all taxi fares are fixed. Trips after 10 pm and before 6 am cost an additional 50%. Taxis can be dispatched at the airport and called from hotels. You'll also find plenty of cabs available near the **Circus** in Basseterre. For four people, here's a sampling of fares:

Airport to Basseterre . . . . US $6
Airport to Frigate Bay . . . . US $10
Airport to Sandy Point. . . . . US $14

Island Tours

Guided island tours are a good way for first-time visitors to enjoy an overview of the islands. You can hire a taxi driver for a personalized tour or call one of these tour companies.

ISLAND TOUR COMPANIES	
Kris Fix It and Tours	☎ (869) 465-4042
TDC Tours	☎ (869) 465-5978
Tropical Tours	☎ (869) 465-4767
Gregg's Safaris	☎ (869) 465-4121

St. Kitts

Orientation

St. Kitts is shaped somewhat like a guitar – or to be less glamorous, a chicken drumstick. The skinny stretch is the **Southeast Peninsula**, a region that's largely undeveloped (at least for now; plans are in the works for a major hotel to make its home on these pristine beaches) and the perfect place for bird-watching, monkey-spotting, and strolling beaches that have no other sign of human life. Birders find the **Great Salt Pond**, **Little Salt Pond** and **Majors Bay Pond** are good sites.

The Southeast Peninsula meets the main part of the island at steep **Sir Timothy's Hill**. On each side of this steep hill (which is flanked by an excellent scenic overlook on which to pull over and get a good view of both the Caribbean and the Atlantic at the same time) lies **Frigate Bay. North Frigate Bay** is on the Caribbean side while Frigate Bay lies on the Atlantic side. The Frigate Bay stretch has many hotel accommodations and guest services and much of the available watersports activities.

Basseterre, the capital of St. Kitts, is a charming waterfront community that bustles with activity on market days and is home to many buildings constructed in the traditional West Indian style.

From Basseterre, the main road travels northwest through many small communities and over many ghuts, which are natural draws from which heavy rains can run off Mount Liamuiga and into

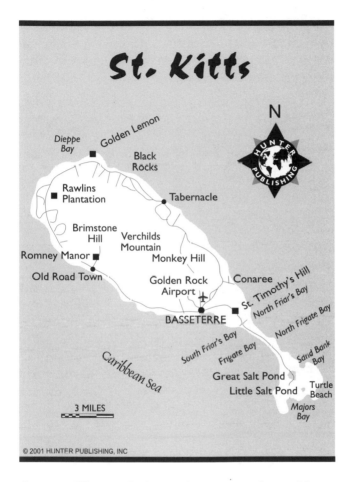

the sea. The road skirts the mountain and hugs the coastline with turnoffs for attractions such as **Romney Manor**, the home of a batik factory; some beautiful grounds at the edge of the rain forest; and the **Carib petroglyphs**.

About two-thirds up the island is the turn for **Brimstone Hill Fortress**, one of the most formidable structures in the Caribbean and a mandatory stop on any island tour.

On the north side of the island lies **Rawlins Plantation** and the **Golden Lemon**, a former plantation with a beautiful black sand volcanic beach. In this part of St. Kitts, long vistas across acres of crops are common sights.

On the east side of the island the views are often of the Caribbean Sea. Here **Ottley's Plantation Inn** draws visitors and offers sweeping views across historic grounds that back up to the rain forest.

One of the most unusual sights in St. Kitts is the **Sugar Train**, a narrow-gauge railroad. A small engine pulls the open-air cars through the fields of sugar cane, picking up the harvest and eventually delivering it to the factory in **Needsmust**. Look out in the fields as you exit **Bradshaw International Airport** for a peek at the train; it's also visible in the fields at several points around the island.

 # Best Places to Stay

The Alive! Price Scale

We've based these estimates on high season for a standard room for two persons (US dollars).

Deluxe . . . . $300+
Expensive . . . . $201-$300
Moderate . . . . $100-$200
Inexpensive . . . . Under $100

Resorts & Hotels

**JACK TAR VILLAGE ROYAL
ST. KITTS BEACH RESORT & CASINO**
Frigate Bay, Basseterre
☎ (869) 465-8651; fax (869) 465-1031
Reservations: ☎ (800) 999-9182
www.allegroresorts.com
Moderate to Expensive

Renovated after Hurricane Luis, this all-inclusive resort is recommended for vacationers looking for activity. Home of the country's only casino, the resort offers plenty of organized fun and evening entertainment as well as a golf course. The fun comes in an all-inclusive package, so all activities, along with food and drink, are included in the price. Although it is not located directly on the beach, it's just a short walk to the sand and surf.

Jack Tar is a favorite with families.

The cool, tile-floor rooms include air conditioning, cable TV, and telephone. As a clue to the resort's fun level, the pools are termed the "quiet pool" and the "rowdy pool." The latter is where you might witness chug-a-lug contests, bingo, or pool volleyball. Other guest facilities include golf, tennis, bicycling, fishing in the lagoon, nightly entertainment, casino action, two restaurants and several bars, a gift shop, and a duty free shop.

St. Kitts

FORT THOMAS HOTEL
Fortlands Street, Basseterre
☎ (869) 465-2695; fax (869) 465-7518
Inexpensive to Moderate

The Fort Thomas Hotel has a good central location. Located in walking distance of downtown Basseterre, the Fort Thomas Hotel has recently refurbished guest rooms, as well as one of the island's largest swimming pools. Facilities include a restaurant and bar, the Olympic-size swimming pool, tennis and table tennis, and a beach shuttle.

OCEAN TERRACE INN
Fisherman's Wharf, Basseterre
☎ (869) 465-2754; fax (869) 465-1057
Reservations: ☎ (800) 524-0512
www.oceanterraceinn.net
Moderate to Expensive

This hotel combines the convenience of a downtown property with the relaxing feel of a resort. Just a short walk from Fisherman's Wharf Restaurant (a property under the same ownership), Ocean Terrace Inn, or OTI, is a favorite with returnees to St. Kitts and with business travelers. The hotel has views of Basseterre Bay and Nevis; many of the recently renovated guest rooms overlook a pool with a swim-up bar and a hot tub. Beautiful landscaping and walks made of stone divided with low-growing grass connect the hotel with two bars. Visitors can take a complimentary shuttle to Turtle Bay on the island's Southeast Peninsula for a day of watersports and beach fun, and then enjoy an evening at the hotel that might include a solo guitarist in the Harbour View Restaurant or a show by the Coronets Steel Orchestra on Friday nights.

OTI offers special packages for adventure travelers. An Eco-Safari package includes seven nights accommodation, transfers, a half-day rain forest tour, a historic sugar and coffee plantation tour, a daily beach shuttle, sunset cruise, and more.

The Ocean Terrace is centrally located.

Plantation Inns

If you're looking for peace and quiet, St. Kitts' plantation inns offer good getaways and a chance to immerse yourself in more of the local atmosphere.

These small inns, built around historic great houses on former plantations, are intimate properties that only host a handful of guests at a time. As part of just a small group, you'll get to know each other as you would if you were aboard a small cruise. Often the owners of the inn live right on the property, so you'll receive personal attention.

RAWLINS PLANTATION
Mount Pleasant, 45 minutes north of Basseterre
☎ (869) 465-6221; fax (869) 465-4954
Reservations: ☎ (800) 346-5358
www.rawlinsplantation.com
Expensive to Deluxe

As far back as 1690, the plantation now known as Rawlins began producing sugar. At the time, the site was one of 50 or 60 estates that produced sugar on the island, using a sail-driven windmill to provide the power to grind the sugar. Nearly 300 years later, the great house, burned in an early fire, was reconstructed and opened as an

St. Kitts

inn. Today, Rawlins is in the hands of Cordon Bleu-trained chef Claire Rawson and her husband, Paul. The windmill remains as a reminder of that early history and today the 300-year-old structure makes a romantic honeymoon suite.

The Rawlins Plantation is known for its romantic atmosphere.

Along with dining, the chief activity around here is pure relaxation. With no phones or televisions in the 10 guest rooms, the emphasis is on leisure. The most romantic of the hideaway rooms is the honeymoon suite, housed in the sugar mill. Guests climb a winding stair from the downstairs living room to the upstairs bedroom perch, its walls made of volcanic stone. Facilities include a grass tennis court, croquet, a pool, and crater and rain forest hikes. Breakfast and dinner are included in the plan as well as afternoon tea and laundry service.

GOLDEN LEMON INN AND VILLAS
Station Street, Dieppe Bay
☎ (869) 465-7260; fax (869) 465-4019
Reservations: ☎ (800) 633-7411
www.goldenlemon.com
Expensive

Fine dining and elegant accommodations lead travelers to the Golden Lemon, located on a black volcanic sand beach in the shadow of the island's volcano. One of the island's finest plantation inns, the Golden Lemon is owned and managed by former *House and Garden* decorating editor Arthur Leaman. The former New Yorker's sense of style shows in every room of the inn, from a great room where guests congregate to the open-air dining area and the immaculate guest rooms.

The property is composed of a 17th-century great house and 15 contemporary seaside villas, each filled with West Indian antiques and an atmosphere that invites relaxation. Suites offer plunge pools just a step from the living room door. The hotel is 15 minutes from Basseterre, and most guests rent cars for their stay.

A historic atmosphere and fine dining are offered at the Golden Lemon.

Facilities include an excellent restaurant and a tennis court. Snorkeling is available on the reef. No children under 18 years of age are allowed.

OTTLEY'S PLANTATION INN
Ottley's Estate, Basseterre, 10 miles north of airport (mailing address: PO Box 345, Basseterre)
☎ (869) 465-7234; fax (869) 465-4760
Reservations: ☎ (800) 772-3039
www.ottleys.com
Expensive to Deluxe

Legend has it that this 18th-century great house is haunted, but that doesn't stop the vacationers who come here looking for peace and quiet. Guest rooms in the great house and in nearby cottages are nestled on 35 acres of tropical grounds. Along with golf and tennis, guests can explore a small rain forest on the grounds and search for vervet monkeys. The inn includes a restaurant and swimming pool.

> ### ⊚ AUTHOR'S TIP
>
> Don't miss the half-mile rain forest trail. Mornings and late afternoons offer the best chance of spotting a monkey.

St. Kitts

Condominiums

HORIZON VILLAS RESORT
Fort Tyson, Frigate Bay
☎ (869) 465-0584; fax (869) 465-0785
Reservations: ☎ (800) 830-9069
Moderate to Expensive

You'll feel as though you have found your home on this beautiful island during a stay in these lovely villas. Perched up on a hillside with a path down to a crescent-shaped beach, the villas are comfortable, cozy, and maintained by a friendly staff. Guest facilities include a pool and a lovely little strip of beach.

Villas

Villas are available for rent by the week, month or longer. The majority of them are managed by agencies.

CARIBVILLAS
☎ (869) 466-4446 or (869) 465-4100

This company handles several villas from two- to four-plus bedrooms. Most offer a pool and some offer a cook and house staff. Visit its website, www.caribvillas.com for rate information and villa specifics.

CARIBBEAN DESTINATIONS
☎ (504) 834-7026 or (800) 888-0897

Offers one- to four- bedroom villas. Most have pool and beach access. No children are allowed in these villas. For more information, visit their website, www.caribbeandest.com.

HALF MOON BAY VILLAS
☎ (869) 465-6705

Manages several villas with full kitchens, cable TV, optional swimming pool, hot tub, and many more features. Visit www.halfmoonbayvillas.com for a full amenity list, rates, and other information.

Small Hotel

BIRD ROCK BEACH HOTEL
Frigate Bay, Basseterre
☎ (869) 465-8914; fax 869-465-1675
Reservations: ☎ (800) 621-1270
Moderate to Expensive

Scuba divers especially enjoy Bird Rock, a property just five minutes from the airport or from Basseterre. The hotel is home of St. Kitts Scuba (☎ 869-465-1189) and divers can head right off the dock on the dive boat. The hotel is simple and clean and rooms include cable TV, air conditioning, telephone, and balcony or patio. Facilities include a restaurant, dockside BBQ grill, pool, bars, tennis, and fitness center.

Bird Rock has good snorkeling along the rocks and diving at the end of the 100-foot dock.

Best Places to Eat

In the restaurant department, you're bound to find something you like here, whether your

St. Kitts

tastes run toward fresh island seafood or cuisines from around the world. Some of the island's restaurants have received accolades over the last few years and gained quite a following among the many returning guests who frequent the island; others are new on the scene. Some restaurants are especially suited for couples looking for a special night out; others welcome families looking for dishes to please even the pickiest eater in the group.

A meal in St. Kitts usually means traditional Caribbean fare such as snapper, grouper, salt fish or even flying fish accompanied by side dishes such as breadfruit, pumpkin, yams, and the obligatory rice and pigeon peas. Everything will be flavorful and often spicy.

Wash down dinner with the local beer, Carib, or the island's own liqueur, Cane Spirit Rothschild, or CSR. Made from cane, this clear liqueur was developed by France's Baron de Rothschild and is manufactured in Basseterre. A popular drink in St. Kitts is "Ting with a zing." Ting is a carbonated grapefruit drink sold throughout the Caribbean. In St. Kitts it is mixed with CSR to create an adult concoction.

The Alive Price Scale (US $)

Includes a drink, tax and tip.

Expensive. . . . . $40+ per person
Moderate . . . . $25-$40
Inexpensive . . . . Under $25

Caribbean Cuisine

FISHERMAN'S WHARF
Fortlands, Basseterre
☎ (869) 465-2754
Inexpensive-Moderate

Relax in the informal seaside atmosphere at this open-air restaurant featuring local dishes. The restaurant itself is located on a wharf and offers romantic views of Basseterre at night. Live entertainment featuring local musicians and dancers make this a happening place.

Continental Cuisine

GOLDEN LEMON
Station Street, Dieppe Bay
☎ (869) 465-7260
Moderate-Expensive

One of the island's best, this elegant restaurant is located on the patio of the Golden Lemon Plantation Inn. A wide variety of dishes, fresh ingredients, and an atmosphere that makes you feel like you're a guest in someone's beautiful tropical home make this a good choice.

ROYAL PALM RESTAURANT
Ottley's Plantation, 10 miles north of airport
☎ (869) 465-7234
Moderate-Expensive

Dine poolside at the Royal Palm Restaurant, located across the lawn from the great house. Diners often begin with an appetizer of conch frit-

St. Kitts

Royal Palm specials include: herbed tenderloin of prime beef, pan-seared red snapper.

ters. Lunch favorites include lobster quesadillas, shrimp ceviche, and flying fish fillet. The dinner selections are more elegant and equally tasty.

RAWLINS PLANTATION
Mount Pleasant, 45 minutes north of Basseterre
☎ (869) 465-6221
Moderate-Expensive

Guests and non-guests stop by Rawlins Plantation for the daily West Indian lunch buffet. The buffet features local favorites such as saffron rice, curried chicken, and flying fish fritters, followed by soursop sorbet. The dishes are prepared using fresh seafood and herbs and vegetables from the garden.

TURTLE BEACH BAR AND GRILL
Southeast Peninsula at Turtle Beach, Basseterre
☎ (869) 465-9086
Inexpensive

Located where the end of the island meets the sea, this laid-back bar and restaurant serves lunch daily and dinner on Saturday. Seafood and island barbecue are specialties. On Sunday afternoon, enjoy a buffet and sounds of the local steel band. Always offered is a great view of Nevis.

Sunup to Sundown

Beaches

There are several beaches on the Southeast Peninsula that have recently become accessible to visitors because of the construction of a new road. These beaches are quite clean and very beautiful and include Sand Bank Bay, Friar's Bay South, and Turtle Beach.

Sand Bank Bay

This beach's seclusion and natural beauty make it an ideal spot for an afternoon adventure. On the northern side of the Southeast Peninsula, five miles east of Basseterre on Dr. Kennedy Simmonds Highway.

South Friar's Bay

The calm water here is optimum for a quiet afternoon. Coconut trees and the beautiful sand provide for magnificent scenery. On the southern side of the Southeast Peninsula, four miles east of Basseterre on Dr. Kennedy Simmonds Highway.

Turtle Beach

A nearby restaurant and bar make Turtle Beach a great spot. Get in the mood of the island with

St. Kitts

some local music and beach sports. On the tip of the Southeast Peninsula, about six miles east of Basseterre on Dr. Kennedy Simmonds Highway.

Frigate Bay

With one beach on the Atlantic Ocean and one on the Caribbean Sea, Frigate Bay is perfect for everything from relaxing quietly in the sun, to body surfing and swimming, to watersports. Just three miles southeast of Basseterre.

Scuba Diving

 St. Kitts is fairly new to the diving world and offers divers a world of pristine sites without crowds. We recommend you dive with a professional dive operator.

The most popular sites are on the island's western side in the calmer Caribbean waters, where visibility runs as much as 100 feet. Top spots include:

- ◎ **Black Coral Reef.** This dive site sits 40 to 70 feet below the surface and is best known for its protected black coral.

- ◎ **Bloody Bay Reef.** Located at 60 to 80 feet, this dive site is noted for its healthy undersea life, from anemones to sea fans. A popular fishing site as well, an occasional shark is seen here, the result of chumming. Divers will find several caves in this area.

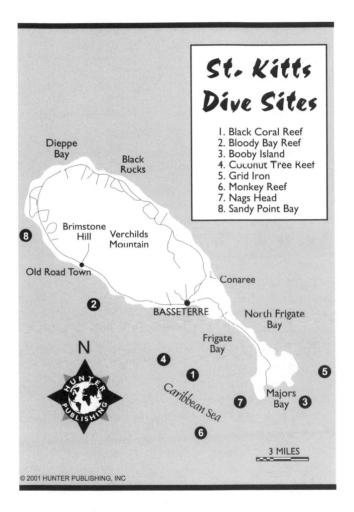

St. Kitts
Dive Sites

1. Black Coral Reef
2. Bloody Bay Reef
3. Booby Island
4. Coconut Tree Reef
5. Grid Iron
6. Monkey Reef
7. Nags Head
8. Sandy Point Bay

Dieppe Bay
Black Rocks
Brimstone Hill
Verchilds Mountain
Old Road Town
Conaree
BASSETERRE
North Frigate Bay
Frigate Bay
Majors Bay
Caribbean Sea
N
3 MILES

© 2001 HUNTER PUBLISHING, INC

⊚ **Booby Island.** This site is in the St. Kitts and Nevis channel, The Narrows, and is for advanced divers because of the current. Jacks and snapper are common here.

St. Kitts

- **Coconut Tree Reef.** A variety of dive experiences, from beginner to advanced, are available on this reef, which starts at 40 feet below the surface before plunging to over 200 feet deep. Beautiful corals and bountiful marine life flourish here.

- **Grid Iron.** Found in the channel between St. Kitts and Nevis, this dive follows an undersea shelf. Look for angelfish as well as rich aquatic life on this dive.

- **Monkey Reef.** You won't see any monkeys down here, but plenty of other life awaits: nurse sharks, stingrays, lobster, and more. This is a shallow dive, approximately 50 feet below the surface off the Southeast Peninsula.

- **Nags Head.** This advanced dive is found where the calm Caribbean Sea meets the rough waters of the Atlantic Ocean. The result is a strong current and rich marine life, including rays, turtles, and more. This dive averages about 80 feet below the sea.

- **Sandy Point Bay.** Over 50 anchors and marine artifacts have been spotted at a section of this site nicknamed "Anchors Away." On other parts of the dive, large basket sponges, jacks, and snappers can be spotted.

Wrecks

As rich as St. Kitts' dive spots are, her wreck sites also attract many underwater enthusiasts. The waters around the islands are dotted with the remains of vessels. Estimates are that 390 ships were sunk off the coast between 1492 and 1825. Some favorite sites includes:

- ◎ *Brassball.* A shallow-water wreck, the *Brassball* lies in just 25 feet of water, making it popular with beginning divers as well as snorkelers and underwater photographers.

- ◎ **MV *Talata*.** Sunk in 1985, this freighter is still in good condition in just 70 feet of water. An intermediate-to-advanced dive, the site is home to many barracudas and large rays.

- ◎ *River Taw.* This 144-foot freighter was sunk about a decade ago and is located just 50 feet below the surface, making it a favorite destination for beginning divers. It is already encrusted with corals and is home to many reef fish.

- ◎ **Tug Boat.** Beginners as well as snorkelers enjoy the tug boat, beached in just 20 feet of water. The site has been popular with many types of marine life, including jacks, grunts, and even a ray or two.

St. Kitts

Dive Operators

Dive operators on St. Kitts can provide instruction, rentals, and transportation to surrounding dive sites. However, most island operators cannot provide a full range of photographic gear rentals and many cannot accept credit cards. Check first.

Kenneth's Dive Centre
Bay Road East
☎ (869) 465-2670 or 465-7043

Ocean Terrace Inn Dive Centre
Ocean Terrace Inn, Basseterre
☎ (869) 465-2754

Pro-Divers
Fisherman's Wharf & Turtle Beach, Fortlands
☎ (869) 465-3223 or (869) 469-9086

St. Kitts Scuba
Basseterre
☎ (869) 465-1189; fax (869) 465-3696

◎ NOTE

There is no hyperbaric chamber in St. Kitts or Nevis; however there are chambers nearby in Puerto Rico and the US Virgin Islands.

Snorkeling

Although these islands are world famous for their scuba diving, many marine attractions can be enjoyed in water just a few feet deep with equipment as limited as a mask and a snorkel.

Just yards from shore, even first time snorkelers can enjoy a look at colorful corals, graceful fans, and fish that include friendly sergeant majors, butterfly fish, and shy damselfish. A top snorkel site is White Bay on the Southeast Peninsula.

> ⊚ **NOTE**
>
> Most dive companies, as well as many hotels, rent dive gear.

Sailing

Whether you want to go out on a day sail, a sunset cruise, or a trip to a neighboring island, it's available from St. Kitts. We enjoyed a catamaran sail to Nevis aboard the *Spirit of St. Kitts*, part of the Leeward Island Charters fleet. It's a scenic ride from Basseterre to Nevis and includes an open bar and a very friendly crew that's happy to point out sights such as the Southeast Peninsula and Booby Island, home to many of the island's feathered species.

St. Kitts

Crewed Sailboat Excursions

The following companies offer trips, with crew included.

Jazzie II (glass-bottom boat)
☎ (869) 465-3529

Kantours
☎ (869) 465-2098 or 465-3128

Leeward Island Charters (catamarans)
☎ (869) 465-7474

Tropical Dreamer
(glass-bottom catamaran)
☎ (869) 465-8224

Tropical Tours
☎ (869) 465-4039 or 465-4167

Bareboat Charters

For those looking to man the helm, whether you'd like to learn to sail a Sunfish or are an old salt that's ready to try your luck in a competition, the **St. Kitts and Nevis Boating Club** has an activity for you. Every other month the club sponsors a day of fun with races, relays, and lessons. For details and dates, contact the St. Kitts and Nevis Boating Club, PO Box 444, Basseterre, St. Kitts, West Indies, ☎ (869) 465-8035; fax (869) 465-8236.

Windsurfing

Windsurfing aficionados will find real challenges here. Dedicated boarders occasionally race between St. Kitts and Nevis. You will find equipment and instruction at the large properties as well as at these operators:

St. Kitts Scuba
Bird Rock Beach Hotel
Frigate Bay
☎ (869) 465-1189

Tropical Surf
Turtle Beach
☎ (869) 465-2380

Blue Water Safari
Princess Street, Basseterre
☎ (869) 466-4933

Horseback Riding

Equestrian lovers will find varied experiences on St. Kitts. Beginners, intermediate, and advanced riders, as well as children aged three and up, can take a beach romp with **Trinity Stables,** ☎ (869) 465-3226 or 465-1446; fax (869) 465-9460. Headquartered near the Jack Tar Village, this operation gives guided rides on the Atlantic beach at your own pace for US $20 per hour. For US $35, experience a three-hour-plus trip to the rain forest with a guide. Departures head up to the rain forest area by jeep, then transfer to horseback for a guided ride through this lush forest.

Parasailing

There is limited parasailing on St. Kitts. Check with these operators:

Fantasy Parasailing
Bentels Drive, Bird Rock
☎ (869) 466-8930

St. Kitts Scuba
Bird Rock Beach Hotel, Frigate Bay
☎ (869) 465-1189

Blue Water Safari
Princess Street, Basseterre
☎ (869) 466-4933

Fishing

Deep-sea fishing is a popular sport in St. Kitts; top catches include tuna, shark, wahoo, snapper and kingfish. You can make arrangements to go out on a half- or full-day charter through most hotels or call:

Kenneth's Dive Centre
Bay Road East, Basseterre
☎ (869) 465-2670 or (869) 465-7043

Ocean Terrace Inn
Basseterre
☎ (869) 465-2754

Tropical Tours
☎ (869) 465-4039 or (869) 465-4167

Golf

There are two golf courses on St. Kitts. Test your skills at the **Golden Rock Golf Club**, ☎ (869) 465-8103, a nine-hole course near the airport. Golden Rock sponsors a day of fun on the last Sunday of every month. The **Royal St. Kitts Golf Course**, ☎ (869) 465-8339, in Frigate Bay adjacent to the Jack Tar was designed by five-time British Open Champion Peter Thompson. The 18-hole course stretches across the peninsula just beyond the all-inclusive resort. Fees range from US $35-$40 for one or two players and use of the practice range is free.

Tennis

Tennis buffs will find courts at the **Jack Tar Village** near Frigate Bay. Day passes are available for non-guests; ☎ (869) 465-8651. Two local clubs also invite guests: the **St. Kitts Bridge and Tennis Club** at Fortlands in Basseterre, ☎ (869) 465-2938; and the **St. Kitts Lawn Tennis Club**, Victoria Road, Basseterre, ☎ (869) 465-2051.

St. Kitts

History Tours

For a look at the plantation history of the island, visitors can take a full-day Plantation Safari with **Gregg's Safaris**, ☎ (869) 465-4121. The mostly off-road trip explores the windward coast plantations and includes the West Indian buffet at Rawlins Plantation. Learn more about the island's coffee, sugar, and cotton industries on this guided trip.

Nature Tours

Both companies listed below offer half- and full-day tours of the rain forest and full day trips to the rim of the volcano.

Kriss Tours
☎ (869) 465-4042

Gregg's Safaris
☎ (869) 465-4121

Island Sightseeing

There's a day's worth of sightseeing on St. Kitts, more if you're especially interested in historic sites. Budget a day for an overall look at the sights, which range from historic homes and museums to natural formations and Indian petroglyphs.

Brimstone Hill

BRIMSTONE HILL FORTRESS NATIONAL PARK

Main Road, between Half-Way Tree and Sandy Point Town in the Parish of St. Thomas
☎ (869) 465-2609/6211

One of the top historical attractions in the Caribbean is Brimstone Hill. Nicknamed "The Gibraltar of the West Indies," it is one of the most amazing stes in the Caribbean, and a mandatory stop for anyone interested in military history. From over 800 feet above sea level, you'll enjoy one of the best views found on any of the islands. On a clear day, you can view Nevis, Montserrat, Saba, St. Martin, and St. Barts.

Brimstone Hill is named for the faint sulfur smell sometimes encountered here.

Made of volcanic stone, the structure took over a century to construct.

At this site, the French and the British fought for control of the island, a battle first won by the French and the next year won back by the British.

Wear good walking shoes and bring along drinking water for your look at Brimstone Hill.

At the parking level, you'll find a small concession that sells water, sodas & snacks.

Your first stop should probably be the Visitors Orientation Centre. Here, you'll see a brief film that gives an overview of the site and its rich history.

From the parking level, walk up the cobbled path to the citadel. Here a view of up to 70 miles makes neighboring islands seem just a stone's (or a cannonball's) throw away. From this lofty peak, it's

St. Kitts

easy to imagine the British forces keeping an eye on the seas over two centuries ago.

The citadel has two levels. A museum featuring Amerindian artifacts, British and French memorabilia, and St. Kitts items is located in the stone rooms. Visitors can climb upstairs for additional views.

⚠ WARNING

Watch young children in the higher areas as there are no railings.

Walking Tour of Basseterre

The capital of St. Kitts and Nevis has had a rough time. Hurricanes, earthquakes, floods, fires, you name it, Basseterre has had it. Nonetheless, the city has come back each time and rebuilt. Today you'll find many historic sites in the city.

THE CIRCUS
Fort and Bank streets
Basseterre

Yes, the circus is in town. This roundabout, modeled after Piccadilly Circus in London, is one of the most photographed sites on the island and is the heart of the city. In the center of the circus sits the **Berkeley Memorial Clock**, a popular meeting place. The green tower holds four clocks, one facing each direction and is named for the Honorable T.B.H. Berkeley, a local planter and politician.

ST. GEORGE'S ANGLICAN CHURCH
Nevis Street
Basseterre

This church is just a short walk from The Circus. Constructed in 1670, it was first named Notre Dame. Burned by the British in 1706, the church was rebuilt, only to be destroyed by an earthquake and then two more times by fire. The Kittitians are persistent folks, though, and in 1869 they built the present church. Nearby, a cemetery dates back as far as the early 1700s.

INDEPENDENCE SQUARE
Basseterre

Stroll through this square near The Circus. This historic site was built in 1790 and first used for slave auctions. It was renamed in 1983 to celebrate the independence of the islands from Great Britain.

Brewery

CARIB BEER BREWERY
West Cayon Street
Basseterre
☎ (869) 465-2309

This plant – also located in Basseterre – offers a tour and complimentary tasting, by appointment only.

St. Kitts

Just Outside of Town

PETROGLYPHS
Six miles northwest of Basseterre,
near Romney Manor

Don't miss the petroglyphs, carved many years
ago by the Carib Indians. While you're stopped
here, check out the handicrafts sold next door by a
neighbor who creates turtles and bird feeders
from coconut shells.

CARIBELLE BATIK
Sx miles northwest of Basseterre,
near Romney Manor
☎ (869) 465-6253

This stop is worth making even if you don't want
to shop. Here you can watch the process of making
batik and buy the finished product in the form of
shirts, wraps, and wall hangings.

BATIK

Batik is an ancient process that uses dyes
and wax to create fantastic designs on fabric. Artisans first paint wax on the fabric,
leaving some areas bare; these are the
patches that will absorb the dye. Small
cracks in the wax give each piece a unique
pattern – no two pieces of batik are the
same.

It's worth a trip to nearby Romney Manor just to
visit the ruins of the stately great house and the

grounds shaded by trees that date back hundreds of years. The closest thing that St. Kitts has to a botanical garden, these grounds are home to many tropical plant species. You can't miss the huge Saman tree, said to be the largest tree in the Caribbean.

On the drive to Caribelle Batik, look for the historic aqueducts along the side of the road, a vestige of the island's early water system.

Southeast Peninsula

Once the last Kittitian frontier, this remote peninsula is now accessible by a modern highway. Some of St. Kitts' most beautiful sights – White House Bay, South Friar Bay, Anthony's Peak – and beaches are located along this area, which is also home to many vervet monkeys. (Look for them in the early mornings and late evenings.) **Turtle Beach** is the most popular beach on the peninsula (actually the only one where you might have a little company). On the drive to the peninsula, you'll pass a salt pond with a distinct pink hue, the result of many tiny kroll shrimp. Birders will enjoy this region for its unspoiled opportunities to spot some of the island's species.

Shop Till You Drop

In Basseterre, duty-free devotees will find plenty of selection at **Pelican Mall** on the waterfront. This two-story mall, designed with Kittitian architecture and tropical colors, features duty-free shops selling everything from china to liquor to Cuban cigars.

St. Kitts

Twenty-six shops make this a popular stop, especially for cruise-ship passengers who come in from the new cruise-ship dock adjacent.

Hours vary by shop, but you can expect most stores to open Monday through Saturday from 8 m until noon, then again from 1 until 4 in the afternoon.

◎ NOTE

The majority of shops are closed on Thursday afternoons.

Fine Jewelry

GLASS ISLAND LIMITED
Princess and Fort Streets, Basseterre
☎ (869) 466-6771

All items for sale in this shop are made on the premises. Here you can find jewelry, dishes and other glass items.

Books

WALL'S DELUXE RECORD AND BOOK SHOP
Fort Street, Basseterre
☎ (869) 465-2159

Find the newest releases in books and music at this popular shop. Also available are guidebooks, local newspapers, and postcards.

China, Crystal & Figurines

ASHBURRY'S
Liverpool Row, Basseterre
☎ (869) 465-8175

Find duty-free items from Royal Doulton, Phillippe Charriol, Princess Marcella Borghese, and other big names. Also sells leather items from Fendi.

Grog, Spirits & Cigars

SMOKES 'N BOOZE
Pelican Mall, Basseterre
☎ (869) 465-2631

Top-brand liquor and tobacco are available here at low prices. Shoppers can even find the Cuban cigars (just make sure not to bring them back to the US!).

> ### 🌀 NOTE
>
> Remember, Americans cannot legally bring Cuban cigars into the United States. It is legal to enjoy them while in the islands.

Local Crafts & Souvenirs

ISLAND HOPPER
The Circus, Basseterre
☎ (869) 465-2905

St. Kitts

This popular store carries many local crafts that capture the culture of the island. They offer gifts for friends at home or a souvenir for yourself!

After Dark

Bars

TROPICS DISCO
Jack Tar Resort, Basseterre
☎ (869) 465-8651

There is no cover charge at this disco, making it a local favorite. Drinks are included for guests of the resort.

PIANO BAR
Jack Tar Resort, Basseterre
☎ (869) 465-8651

Open from 5 pm to 1:30 am, this bar serves up local favorites, soft drinks, or your preferred drink.

THE TERRACE BAR
The Ocean Terrace Inn, Basseterre
☎ (869) 465-2754

Open in the evenings, this is a great place to relax and watch the sunset over the harbor.

Cinema

MOVIES III
Bay Road East, Basseterre
☎ (869) 465-0908

St. Kitts A-Z

Amex

American Express Office
Liverpool Row, Basseterre
☎ (869) 465-2098

Banks

Bank of Nova Scotia
Fort Street, Basseterre
☎ (869) 465-4141

Development Bank of St. Kitts and Nevis
Church Street, Basseterre
☎ (869) 465-2288

Royal Bank of Canada
Wellington Road, Basseterre
☎ (869) 465-2259

Barclays Bank
The Circus, Basseterre
☎ (869) 465-2519

Consulates

There are no consulates on St. Kitts.

Dentists

Dr. Keith Blake and Associates
South Independence Square, Basseterre
☎ (869) 465-9197

Seventh Day Adventist Dental Clinic
East Park Range, Basseterre
☎ (869) 465-8174

Emergency Phone Numbers

Police .... ☎ 911
Fire........................... ☎ 333
Ambulance..................... ☎ 911
Police Information Line......... ☎ 707

Grocery Stores

Brookes Shopping Centre
Fort Thomas Road, Basseterre
☎ (869) 465-7673

Hyperbaric Chamber

There is no hyperbaric chamber on St. Kitts; the nearest facilities are on Saba or St. Thomas.

Hospitals

Hospital Molineux
Cardin Avenue, Johnson Village
☎ (864) 465-7398

JN France General Hospital
St. Johnson Village, Basseterre
☎ (869) 466-6681

Optical Services

Caribbean Optical Eye Clinic
West Independence, Basseterre
☎ (869) 466-3937

Pharmacies

Parris Pharmacy LTD
Central Street, Basseterre
☎ (869) 465-8596

Photo Labs

Willett's Photo Studio
Amory's Mall, Cayon Street, Basseterre
☎ (869) 465-2593

Places of Worship

Church of Christ
Cunningham, Basseterre
☎ (869) 465-1372

Church of Jesus Christ of Latter Day Saints
Shadwell Site, Basseterre
☎ (869) 465-7767

Methodist Church Annex
Seaton Street, Basseterre
☎ (869) 465-2346

St. Kitts

Post Offices

Basseterre . . . . ☎ (869) 462-2521
Cayon . . . . ☎ (869) 465-7208
Dieppe Bay . . . . ☎ (869) 465-7367

Room Tax

A 7% room tax, plus 10% service charge will be added to your hotel bill.

Telephone Service

International Directory Inquiries. . ☎ 412
Local Directory Inquires . . . . ☎ 411

Website

www.stkitts-nevis.com.

Nevis

It's a quick trip from St. Kitts to Nevis but the distance is measured in far more than miles. Nevis is almost a step back in time, to days before mass tourism and jet service. On this quiet cousin to St. Kitts, you'll find that the pace is slow and living is easy.

The island was first named Oualie (pronounced Wally) by the Carib Indians, a word that means land of beautiful water, an appropriate moniker. The island's 9,000 residents are outnumbered two-to-one by wild vervet monkeys, so nightlife on this charming isle often consists of watching raiding marauders sneak out from the lush cover of the bush and steal fruits on the hotel grounds.

Nevis is one of the Caribbean's best destinations for the eco-tourist. Rain forest hikes, birding, volcano hikes, and plenty of flora and fauna make this island especially popular with nature lovers.

Transportation

Newcastle Airport is the port of entry for many Nevis visitors. The small airport is currently undergoing expansion so that it will be able to accommodate larger aircraft. Currently, it is served by seven-minute flights from St. Kitts. See *Getting Here*, pages 128-9, for complete details about airlines and ferry companies servicing Nevis.

Getting Around the Island

Car & Jeep Rentals

Rental cars are available on Nevis, but be advised that driving is on the left side of the road. A visitor's license is available from the **Police Traffic Department** for EC $50. Located in Newcastle, a quarter-mile from the airport. ☎ (869) 469-9326.

Car rentals, from small cars to jeeps, are available from several companies. Rental rates average about US $40-$45 for a mid-size and US $45 for a jeep.

CAR RENTAL COMPANIES	
Gajor's Car Rental	☎ (869) 469-5367/1439
Nisbett's Car Rental	☎ (869) 469-9211
Noel's Car Rental	☎ (869) 469-5199
Parry's Car Rentals	☎ (869) 469-5917
Skeete's Car Rental	☎ (869) 469-9458
Stanley's Car Rental	☎ (869) 469-1597
Striker's Car Rental	☎ (869) 469-2654
TDC Rentals Ltd.	☎ (869) 469-6999

Driving Tips

In British tradition, traffic keeps to the left side of the road. This can be confusing on your first day behind the wheel, so start off a little slower than usual. Most cars are right-hand drive and will therefore necessitate a few adjustments (on our first excursion we turned on the windshield wipers every time we tried to give a turn signal!).

> **⚠ WARNING**
>
> On Nevis and in rural areas of St. Kitts, lookout for wildlife and livestock: you'll be sharing the roads with monkeys, donkeys and goats!

Taxis & Mini-Buses

Excellent taxi and mini-bus service is available on Nevis. The following chart offers sample rates from Newcastle Airport and from Charlestown. Add an additional 50% to hire a taxi between 10 pm and 6 am; add 20% extra to arrange a taxi after 6 pm.

Newcastle Airport to:

Charlestown	US $11
Four Seasons Resort	$11
Golden Rock Estate	$15
Hermitage	$15
Montpelier Plantation	$17
Nisbet Plantation Inn	$6

Charlestown to:

Four Seasons . . . . US $6
Golden Rock Estate $11
Hermitage Plantation $9
Montpelier Plantation $10
Mount Nevis Hotel $14
Newcastle Pottery $14
Nisbet Plantation Inn $13

Call one of the following companies to arrange pick-up.

Ace Taxi Service
Water Front, Charlestown
☎ (869) 469-1973

City Taxi Stand
Main Street, Charlestown
☎ (869) 469-5621

Bicycles

Bicycles are available for rent from **Windsurfing Nevis**, ☎ (869) 464-9682, Oualie Bay.

With its small population and light traffic, Nevis is a great place for cyclists. Touring the island this way is a great way to meet locals.

Bus Service

Bus service is available on the islands. A schedule can be obtained from your hotel desk.

Nevis

Island Tours

First-time visitors to Nevis would do well to take
an island tour for an overview of the island. Although it is small, Nevis is home to many small
villages and a guided look is the best way to learn
more about the rich history of this destination.
Guided tours are available from taxi drivers or
from these tour companies.

ISLAND TOUR COMPANIES	
All Seasons Streamline Tours	☎ (869) 469-1138
Eco-Tours Nevis	☎ (869) 469-2091
Heb's Nature Tours	☎ (869) 469-2501
Scarborough Tours	☎ (869) 465-5429
Sunrise Tours	☎ (869) 469 2758
Top to Bottom	☎ (869) 469-3371
Tropical Tours	☎ (869) 465-4167

Orientation

Getting around Nevis is a simple task – if all
else fails just stay on the "main road" (yes,
that's what people call it) and follow it all the way
around the island to where you started. Most of
the main road follows the coastline, skirting the
steep slopes that lead to Mount Nevis.

From **Charlestown**, the road winds north adjacent to **Pinney's Beach**, one of the island's finest

stretches of sand, and makes its way through the community of **Cotton Ground** and past the **Four Seasons Nevis**, the largest accommodation on the island.

Past Cotton Ground, the road forks, following the coastal path to **Newcastle Airport**, **Oualie Beach** and **Nisbet Plantation** or taking the

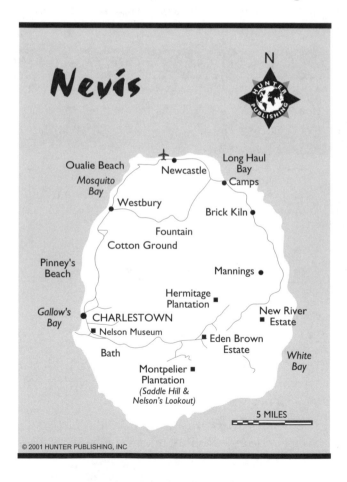

© 2001 HUNTER PUBLISHING, INC

mountainous turn to **Spring Hill**, **Fountain**, and **Mount Lily**.

Both roads meet up on the east side of the island and continue to traditional West Indian communities such as **Brick Kiln**, **Whitehall**, and **Mannings** before turning back across the southern stretch of island. Here the communities line the road, small villages with names like Chicken Stone, Pond Hill, Church Ground and Fig Tree. This region is also home to **The Hermitage Inn** and **Montpelier Plantation**, both in Fig Tree Parish.

Best Places to Stay

Room prices vary greatly with the type of accommodation, location, and time of year. High season (mid-December through mid-April) brings prices about 40% higher than in summer months.

The Alive! Price Scale

Prices based on the cost of a double room for two people, per night.

Deluxe . . . . US $300+
Expensive . . . . $201-$300
Moderate . . . . $100-$200
Inexpensive . . . . Under $100

Resorts & Hotels

FOUR SEASONS NEVIS
Pinney's Beach, Charlestown
☎ (869) 469-1111; fax (869) 469-1112
Reservations: ☎ (800) 332-3442 in the US,
☎ (800) 332-3442 in Canada
www.fourseasons.com
Expensive to Deluxe

This resort is the most luxurious accommodation on Nevis and indeed one of the top resorts in the Caribbean. Boasting a championship golf course, 10 tennis courts, two outdoor Jacuzzis, 24-hour room service, and more, this resort is for those looking for a little pampering.

The Four Seasons is a popular choice with honeymooners and lovebirds.

The Four Seasons Nevis sprawls across grounds dotted with coconut palms and other carefully tended fauna. Guests can enjoy a round of golf, scuba, windsurf, or just sun around the pool, cooled by Evian water sprayed on guests by mindful pool attendants.

MOUNT NEVIS HOTEL AND BEACH CLUB
Newcastle, 10 miles north of the airport
☎ (869) 469-9373; fax (869) 469-9375
Reservations: ☎ (800) 75-NEVIS
Moderate

On a tropical island where other resorts boast palm-lined beaches, historic great houses, and guest lists that have included Princess Di, it's not easy to make your mark.

But Mount Nevis Hotel and Beach Club has done it by offering reasonably priced contemporary accommodations, spectacular views and, most of all, gourmet dining. The **Mount Nevis Restaurant**, overlooking the aquamarine waters of the Caribbean and the sister island of St. Kitts, is highly regarded in the gastronomic world.

Equally appealing as the cuisine are the magnificent views that the restaurant enjoys, of both the sea and the soaring Mount Nevis, which is almost always topped with a cloudy cap that once inspired Columbus to name this island "Our Lady of the Snows." Visitors have no fear of chilly days at this latitude, however, where hours are spent luxuriating in a poolside hammock, down at the beach club on the powdery sand, or hiking along nearby trails where it's not uncommon to spot a vervet monkey in early morning and late afternoon hours.

Rooms here offer a telephone, air conditioning, cable TV, and video players. A pool with a good view of the sea helps travelers cool off on hot days, and the hotel also has a beach facility. The Mount Nevis Beach Club has a restaurant and beach pavilion.

From Mount Nevis Hotel and Beach Club, a one-hour hike up Round Hill to **"Telegraph Tower"** is available to hikers, guests, and non-guests alike. The peak, over 1,000 feet above sea level, affords good views of the island. Other popular hikes are the trails that lead to **Round Hill** and **Cat Ghaut Nature Trail**, which winds among lady orchids, bamboo trees, and, occasionally, some vervet monkeys. Even the hotel's grounds are of interest. The property is located on **Round**

Hill Estate, which was a former citrus grove in the early 1800s. At the edge of the estate's lawn are the ruins of 200-year-old **Cottle Church**, built by Thomas Cottle, Nevis' president in the early 1800s. Early-morning visitors to Cottle Church often encounter clouds of tiny white butterflies or vervet monkeys.

OUALIE BEACH HOTEL
Oualie Bay, a five-minute drive north from airport
☎ (869) 469-9735; fax (869) 469-9176
www.oualie.com
Moderate to Expensive

Oualie (pronounced Wally) is the old Carib Indian name for Nevis and translates as land of beautiful water.

Watersports buffs will find one clear choice on Nevis: Oualie Beach Hotel. Home of Nevis' only dive shop and windsurfing operator, this hotel also offers a fine stretch of sand, 22 charming Caribbean bungalows with screened seaside porches and a comfortable atmosphere.

Oualie makes a good choice for families too. Cribs are available as well as a kids' menu.

Oualie is a great place for families!

Windsurfing and scuba diving packages are available. Five days of unlimited windsurfing is offered with a seven-night stay and 10 days of unlimited windsurfing is offered with a 14-day stay. Scuba packages include two dives daily with their NAUI and PADI dive shop. Packages include a five-night stay with three days of diving or a nine-night stay with seven days of diving.

Rooms here are spacious and perfect for quick dashes to the beach. Four units include full kitchens. All rooms include a minibar, hair dryer, electronic safe, direct dial telephone, and cable TV; air conditioning is offered in the Deluxe and studio units. Facilities include diving, deep-sea fishing, windsurfing, and sailing and are available for guests and non-guests alike.

Plantations Inns

GOLDEN ROCK ESTATE
Main Road, Gingerland; 10 miles
southwest of airport
☎ (869) 469-3346; fax (869) 469-2113
Reservations: ☎ (800) 223-9815
www.golden-rock.com
Moderate to Deluxe

This casually elegant inn is a favorite with eco-tourists because of the diligent efforts of its owner/manager, Pam Barry. A fifth-generation Nevisian, Barry emphasizes local culture, history, and nature studies, offering her self-guided nature trails to both guests and non-guests alike. Her efforts have elevated this inn to the position of one of the top Caribbean accommodations for nature lovers.

Early in the morning and late in the afternoon, vervet monkeys come from the surrounding rain forest and entertain guests with their antics.

Tucked in a 96-acre preserve just steps from the thick forest, this inn features 14 rooms housed in seven charming cottages. A sugar mill dating back to 1815 offers a special accommodation for a lucky couple or family of four; the two-story room has two bedrooms (and some say a resident ghost). Public areas are housed in historic stone buildings. Most rooms are fairly simple, featuring locally made furniture.

Golden Rock is a top choice for eco-travelers.

But the real beauty of Golden Rock lies in its garden-like setting, where flowering plants and trees make this site as beautiful as a botanical garden.

Special learning vacations emphasizing history and culture, watercolor painting, or nature studies are offered periodically; call for details.

MONTPELIER PLANTATION INN
Montpelier Estate, 25 minutes west of the airport
☎ (869) 469-3462; fax (869) 469-2932
www.montpeliernevis.com
Expensive

Montpelier is closed annually from late August through early October.

Travelers may have heard of this classic plantation inn because of one of its most famous guests: the late Princess Diana. When Diana and her children visited Nevis, they opted for this hotel's quiet seclusion. Both royalty and honeymooners are offered peace and quiet in this very British hotel located on the slopes of Mount Nevis.

Montpelier is one of the island's most elegant inns.

Princess Diana focused the eyes of the world on Montpelier, but it was hardly the property's first brush with royalty. On March 11, 1787, Admiral Horatio Nelson married Fanny Nisbet in front of a royal audience right on these grounds.

Today the plantation includes a 16-room inn that exudes a dignified British air appreciated by travelers who come to the Caribbean for peace and quiet. The inn provides shuttle service to the beaches and evenings here are spent at the open-air restaurant that features classical cuisine with many local ingredients. The rooms are decorated in a tropical style and include a telephone, ceiling fan, hair dryer, tea and coffee maker, and patio;

electricity is 220 volts with a 110 volt shaver adapter. Facilities include a swimming pool, tennis court, restaurant, and bar.

The inn also has a private stretch of beach along Pinney's Beach with lounging facilities. Complimentary transportation to the beach is available daily.

NISBET PLANTATION BEACH CLUB
Main Road, Newcastle, St. James Parish;
five minutes north of the airport
☎ (869) 469 -9325; fax (869) 469-9864
Reservations: ☎ (800) 742-6008
www.nisbetplantation.com
Expensive to Deluxe

This plantation was the former home of Admiral Nelson's bride, Fanny Nisbet. The plantation today is a 38-room inn boasting one of Nevis' most striking vistas: a quarter-mile palm-lined walk from the great house to one of Nevis' finest beaches. Guests stay in lemon-tinted bungalows scattered throughout the property. Today the great house of this former coconut plantation is home to an elegant restaurant and bar. Other facilities include beach, pool, and tennis courts.

The expansion of the Nevis airport onto land near Nisbet has caused some concern for the peace and quiet enjoyed on the resort beach. Time will tell how much effect increased air traffic will have on Nisbet, which enjoys a tranquil atmosphere with an elegant clientele, many of whom travel from England for a two- or three-week respite during winter months.

A HISTORY OF NISBET PLANTATION

On an island of fascinating historic properties, the story of Nisbet is perhaps one of the most captivating. Nisbet takes its name from Dr. Nisbet, the property's first owner. A keystone, found today in the ruins of the windmill in front of the great house, still bears the date 1778 and the family initials. Frances "Fanny" Nisbet was the widow of the doctor and became the wife of Horatio Nelson in 1787. For years, Nisbet Estate was run as a sugar plantation and later as a coconut plantation.

Eventually, the property fell into the hands of Mary Pomeroy, daughter of one of the Knights of Malta. Fiesty Mary Pomeroy had married into another lofty Maltese family through an arranged marriage. One night, she didn't like something her husband said from the other end of the table and threw a plate of pudding at him. Walking out, she never returned. During World War II, Mary was rumored to be a spy; after the war she moved to England to take up interior decorating.

In the late 1940s, Mary Pomeroy's life took a drastic turn when a truck carrying steel girders lost part of its load, which fell onto her. She was presumed dead and carried to the morgue, but she revived and demanded to be taken to the hospital. After two years of surgeries, she bought Nisbet in 1950 with her compensation from the accident (at the time the highest ever awarded to anyone in England). Mary eventually began converting rooms in the great house into guest accommodations; then at the end of the decade, she began adding cottages.

With the Anguilla rebellion in 1967, Mary was advised against returning to Nevis and struck a deal with Geoff Boon. He took possession of Nisbet and she took a property in Sint Maarten called Mary's Boon. Geoff Boon was killed in a flying accident in 1978 and Nisbet was purchased by three associates: George Barnum (who later sold the hotel to its present owner), Fred Kelsick (who died in 1988), and Bob Hitchins, the chief pilot of Carib Aviation (who died in a flying accident in 1987).

HERMITAGE PLANTATION INN
Main Road, St. John, Fig Tree Parish, 10 minutes south of airport
☎ (869) 469-3477; fax (869) 469-2481
Reservations: ☎ (800) 742-4276
www.hermitagenevis.com
Expensive

The history of the island is also the emphasis of this charming inn. This mountainside property boasts such a classically Caribbean setting that it's often selected for fashion shoots. This plantation inn is built around a 245-year-old great house. Sprinkled around grounds bursting with tropical blooms stand restored plantation cottages that serve as guest rooms for those looking for the ultimate in privacy.

Guests have access to a swimming pool and tennis courts as well as romantic pursuits such as carriage rides and horseback riding. All rooms include private porches with hammocks, four-poster canopy beds, mini-refrigerators, hair dryers, and ceiling fans.

OLD MANOR ESTATE AND HOTEL
Gingerland, 10 minutes southwest of airport
☎ (869) 469-3445; fax (869) 469-3388
Reservations: ☎ (800) 892-7093
Moderate to Expensive

Plantation inn luxury as well as peace and quiet can be found at Old Manor. This 13-room plantation inn is custom-made for those looking to truly get away from it all. The atmosphere is quiet – really quiet – so book this inn only if you're happy with the sound of a braying donkey for your morning alarm (and with the occasional overhead conversations from nearby rooms). Rooms are large and bright, with white-painted wood walls along with some stone interiors that recall the inn's previous life as a 17th-century sugar plantation. Both rooms and suites are available; select an upstairs unit for soaring ceilings and top views. Although the baths are sorely in need of a facelift, the rooms are comfortable and romantically cozy.

The grounds of Old Manor include ruins of a sugar works, now sprouting with local fauna, and stone ruins that make a good spot to try to visualize a bygone era. Located on the foothills of Mount

Nevis, the inn offers complimentary transportation to its beach facility, **Beachcomber**, on Pinney's Beach. Beachcomber serves an excellent lunch (and a good rum punch) and Pinney's Beach is one of the top stretches of sand on the island. Facilities include a swimming pool with a great view of Mount Nevis, whirlpool (not heated), restaurant and bar, beach bar and beach facilities, complimentary shuttle to beach, and complimentary laundry.

The Old Manor is a perfect place for anyone looking to get away from it all and relax!

Villas

Royal Palm Villas, ☎ (869) 469-0007, offers properties with private porches, cable TV, fax/modem lines, a view of beautiful gardens and many other luxuries. For information on rentals, visit www.royalpalmvillas-nevis.com.

Small Hotels

HURRICANE COVE BUNGALOWS
Main Road, Oualie Beach, five minutes north of airport
☎ (869) 469-9462; fax (869) 469-9462
Moderate to Expensive

Independent travelers looking for the self-sufficiency of a housekeeping unit – as well as some of the most splendid views on the island – will love these stylish bungalows. Each of the 10 hill-hugging cottages was constructed in Scandinavia, broken down and reassembled on a slope overlooking St. Kitts in the distance. Today they're all open-air and furnished with Caribbean artwork. One-, two-, and three-bedroom bungalows with kitchens are available, from which guests can walk down to the beach.

Best Places to Eat

The Alive Price Scale

Expensive . . . . US $40+ per person
Moderate . . . . $25-$40
Inexpensive . . . . Under $25

> ⊚ **NOTE**
>
> Reservations are generally not required, but we recommend you make them for dinner, especially in high season.

Caribbean Cuisine

BEACHCOMBER
Pinneys Beach, Charlestown
☎ (869) 469-5203
Inexpensive

This relaxed beach bar is open for lunch and dinner and features conch chowder, tannin fritters (a burger made of grilled mahi mahi) or grilled fillet of wahoo. The atmosphere here is about as casual as you can get; order your meal then go take a quick dip in the sea if you like. Every Sunday the gift shop hosts a fun fashion show.

Continental Cuisine

THE DINING ROOM
Four Seasons Nevis, Charlestown
☎ (869) 469-1111
Expensive

Although for lunch many visitors to the Four Seasons Nevis select the open-air Grill Room, for a truly elegant meal they move to the great house's dining room. This elegant eatery offers diners a candlelight meal and serves up many local seafood specialties accompanied by an extensive wine list.

Four Seasons specialties: saffron & potato-crusted grouper with Roma tomato and basil salad.

MONTPELIER PLANTATION
Pond Hill, Montpelier, 25 minutes west of airport
☎ (869) 469-3462
Expensive

Evenings begin with a cocktail hour enjoyed in the great room as guests discuss their day while amiable owners James and Celia Gaskell take orders for dinner. Eventually guests make their way to the verandah for an open-air dinner served with elegance and style. Some typical dishes include fillet of mahi mahi with a Swiss cheese crust, breast of duck in soya and ginger, tenderloin of veal, and grilled lobster with Creole hollandaise.

One Montpelier special is curried butternut, sweet potato & cheddar soup.

Although many resorts make the claim, Montpelier is one that truly defines casual elegance and offers a taste of the Caribbean the way it used to be.

MOUNT NEVIS HOTEL & BEACH CLUB
Mount Nevis, Newcastle, 10 miles north of airport
☎ (869) 469-9373
Inexpensive-Moderate

This hillside hotel is well known for its reasonably priced contemporary accommodations, spectacular views, and most of all, gourmet dining. The Mount Nevis Restaurant, overlooking the aquamarine waters of the Caribbean and the sister island of St. Kitts, is highly regarded in gastronomic circles.

Mount Nevis is known for its coconut-fried lobster and island-spiced crème brûlée.

You'll enjoy such specialties as lobster wontons with ginger-soy dipping sauce, grilled snapper with mango and tomatillo salsa, and island-spiced crème brûlée.

COCONUT FRIED LOBSTER
This delicious dish is one of many specialties at Mount Nevis Hotel & Beach Club.

Lobster: 1 lobster tail (12 oz), split, cleaned and deveined; 2 cups shredded unsweetened coconut; 1 cup all-purpose flour; ¼ cup cornstarch; 1 bottle of beer (12 oz); salt, pepper and cayenne to taste.

Sauce: ½ cup diced ripe mango; ¼ cup peeled and diced tomato; 2 tablespoons chopped fresh coriander; 1 tablespoon chopped shallot; ¼ cup dry white wine; ¼ cup fish or chicken stock; 1 tablespoon lemon or lime juice; salt, pepper and cay-enne to taste; 4 tablespoons butter.

Preheat deep fryer to 375°F. Remove lobster meat from shell, leaving tail fan shell portion attached. Place flour, cornstarch, and seasoning in bowl. Whisk beer into flour mixture until smooth and thin in consistency (you may not need all of the beer). Cover and let rest for half-hour.

Prepare the sauce by first placing a small sauté pan over medium-high heat. Add one tablespoon of butter and chopped shallot and sauté for 15 seconds. Add mango and tomato and sauté for 15 additional seconds. Add wine, stock, lemon or lime juice, and coriander, and reduce mixture by half. Whisk in remaining butter and season to taste with salt, pepper and cayenne. Remove from heat; keep warm.

To fry lobster, hold lobster by tail fan shell portion. Dip meat into beer batter, letting excess batter drip off. Dredge batter-coated lobster in coconut until well coated on all sides. Repeat process with other half of lobster tail. Carefully drop lobster tails into deep fry fat and let fry until coating is lightly browned and lobster is cooked through. Remove to paper towels to drain.

Serve lobster tails, whole or sliced, and spoon mango sauce over them. Yields: one serving.

NISBET PLANTATION

Main Road, Newcastle, five minutes north of the airport
☎ (869) 469-9325
Expensive

Nisbet specials include chilled pear and beet soup with light ginger-cinnamon croutons.

The focal point of the resort is the great house, which dates back to the earliest days of the sugar plantation that began in 1778. This two-story great house, with a wide, screened verandah across the back, is a fine restaurant. Start your evening with a drink at the great house bar then step out on the verandah for a memorable meal accompanied by fine wine.

OUALIE BEACH HOTEL

Main Road, Oualie Beach, five minutes north of Charlestown on the main road
☎ (869) 469-9735
Moderate

This casual restaurant features the creations of Chef Patrick Fobert, who combines French recipes with a Caribbean flair. Diners select from chicken mousse filled with Creole conch, roasted rack of lamb in Jamaican jerk crust, tamarind rum-based wahoo filet, and more. Try the panache of soup with pumpkin.

Sunup to Sundown

Nevis offers plenty of sun, sand, and surf, but you'll also find other activities: walking, birding, golfing, hiking, snorkeling, bicycling, fishing, or horseback riding.

Nevis

Beaches

Nevis has several excellent beaches; most are a toasty golden color.

Oualie Beach

This is the most active beach on Nevis, with watersport operations aplenty. Located five miles north of Charleston on the Main Road.

Pinney's Beach

One of the island's best beaches. The waters here are protected by reefs and popular with snorkelers, swimmers, and sunbathers. From Charlestown, head north on Main Street. Turn onto Old Hospital Road, which takes you to the beach.

Scuba Diving

Nevis' sole operator, **SCUBA Safaris**, ☎ (869) 469-9518, fax (869) 469-9619, is at Oualie Beach. Ellis Chaderton, a NAUI instructor and owner of the operation, reports that, "Reefs here are in good shape. They're not overdone and are pretty much virgin territory." SCUBA Safaris, a PADI and NAUI affiliated operator, offers two 32-foot custom-built dive boats that can handle up to 14 divers per boat. Prices are US $45 for a single-tank dive, and $60 for a night dive. Resort courses are also available.

Chaderton notes that there are 40 dive sites in the Nevis vicinity including coral gardens. Most wreck diving is done near Basseterre in St. Kitts. Night dives are also available, a time when five to six turtles are often reported to be seen. Visibility varies by location. Sometimes visibility is not good on the south side of Nevis. Some top dive sites for Nevis vacationers include:

- **Booby Shoals**. This site sits between Cow 'n Calf Rocks and Booby Island. Divers find an abundance of marine life here including stingray, nurse sharks, and lobster. This shallow site is up to 30 feet in depth and can be used by both certified and resort-course divers.

- **Champagne Garden**. Located just minutes from Pinney's Beach, this site is named for the bubbles created by an underwater sulfur vent. With its warm water temperatures, many tropical fish are drawn to this site.

- **Coral Garden**. Two miles west of Pinney's Beach, this coral reef is home to schools of Atlantic spadefish and many large sea fans. With a maximum depth of 70 feet, it's a favorite with both resort-course and certified divers.

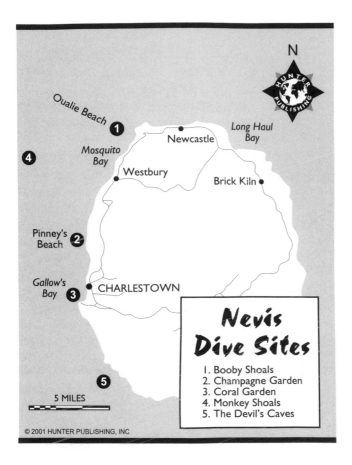

Nevis

Nevis Dive Sites

1. Booby Shoals
2. Champagne Garden
3. Coral Garden
4. Monkey Shoals
5. The Devil's Caves

© 2001 HUNTER PUBLISHING, INC

⊚ **Monkey Shoals**. Two miles west of the Four Seasons Resort Nevis, this reef starts at 40 feet and offers dives of up to 100 feet in depth. Angelfish, turtles, nurse sharks, corals, sea fans, sponges, and sea whips are noted here.

◎ **The Devil's Caves**. Located on the south tip of Nevis, this 40-foot dive has a series of coral grottos and underwater lava tubes. Lobsters, turtles, squirrelfish, and needlefish are seen at this site used by both certified and resort-course divers.

Snorkeling

 Although these islands are world famous for their scuba diving, many marine attractions can be enjoyed in water just a few feet deep with equipment as limited as a mask and a snorkel. Good snorkeling is available just offshore at many locations, but for the best opportunities, visit the shallow-water dive sites, including **Booby Shoals, Nags Head** and **Devil's Caves** (see above).

Snorkel gear is available from **Scuba Safaris** on Oualie Beach; ☎ (869) 469-9518, fax (869) 469-9619.

◎ AUTHOR'S TIP

Operators will supply snorkels, masks, and fins, but you don't really need fins for the snorkel excursions. If you are not an experienced snorkeler, fins can be tough to control and you'll run the risk of kicking (and thereby killing) coral formations.

Nevis

Sailing

A day spent sailing around Nevis can offer beautiful island vistas as well as snorkeling and swimming opportunities along secluded beaches.

Sailboat Operators

Call these operators to arrange an excursion:

Leeward Island Charters
(catamaran sailing)
☎ (869) 465-7474

Nevis Water Sports
(powerboat rentals)
☎ (869) 469-9690

Sea Nevis Charter Boat (day sailing)
☎ (869) 469-1997

Jones Estate
☎ (869) 469-9239 (sailing)

Newcastle Bay Marina Watersports Centre (motor yachts)
☎ (869) 469-9373 or 469-9395

The *Sea Nevis*
☎ (869) 469-1997

Nevis Water Sports
Oualie Beach
☎ (869) 469-9690

Windsurfing

Windsurfers can learn basic skills on the bay at **Oualie Beach**. Advanced surfers can traverse **The Narrows** to St. Kitts, a two-mile passage that's often rough but a favorite with die-hard competitors, or ride the waves and jump the reefs of **Newcastle** and **Nisbet** beaches. **Windsurfing Nevis**, ☎ (869) 469-9735 or (800) 682-5431, offers Bic and Mistral boards (race, slalom, and wave) as well as lessons for any level.

Horseback Riding

Ira Dore's Stable is at the Garner's Estate. You can reach them at ☎ (869) 469-5528, or sign up at your hotel activity desk. Ira Dore's offers a combination trail and beach ride on Saturdays and Sundays. They are located in the Newcastle area of the island. They also teach English-style riding.

The **Nevis Equestrian Centre at Cole Hill**, ☎ (869) 469-8118, offers guided tours of the Saddle Hill area, the historic plantations, Nelson's Lookout, historic Gingerland, and other scenic points. Many of the trails offer good views of neighboring islands.

The Hermitage, ☎ (869) 469-3477, has an equestrian center offering a 1½-hour trail ride through historic Gingerland. Escorted trail rides are English style and taken at the pace of the least-skilled rider. Headgear is provided. For riders over 250 pounds, two Belgian horses are available. Three trails are offered:

- ◎ From Hermitage stable uphill to **Zetland** and **Dunbar estates**, then to **Old Manor** and back to **Cole Hill**.

- ◎ From stable of the old **Morgans estate** to the **Hamilton estate** (cousin of Alexander Hamilton) to **St. John Fig Tree Church** to **Cole Hill**.

- ◎ From stables to **Zetland**, **Old Manor**, **Stoney Ground**, and **Golden Rock**.

Riding lessons are also available at The Hermitage. For those who'd rather let someone else take the reins, plantation **carriage rides** are offered. The relaxing two- or three-mile ride travels through historic Gingerland on hilly backroads where vacationers can witness traditional West Indian life. The carriages are authentic Creole adaptations of mid-19th century Victorian styles and are constructed of West Indian mahogany.

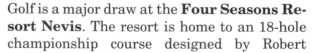

Fishing

Deep-sea excursions are available from **Oualie Beach**, ☎ (869) 469-9735. Available year-round.

Golf

Golf is a major draw at the **Four Seasons Resort Nevis**. The resort is home to an 18-hole championship course designed by Robert

Trent Jones II. Perched on a slope of Mount Nevis, the course affords good views of neighboring St. Kitts. For information, ☎ (869) 469-1111.

Tennis

The top tennis spot on the island is the **Four Seasons Resort Nevis**, home to a Peter Burwash International tennis program. Professional coaches assist with lessons and competitions; many courts are lighted for night play. Non-guests can play here for US $15 per court, per hour, and they may also participate in round-robin tournaments. ☎ (869) 469-1111.

Unique Tours

Many visitors spending a week or more on Nevis take a day trip to one of the neighboring islands. It's a quick hop by air to St. Kitts for a day of touring or hiking. Service between St. Kitts and Nevis is available on **Air St. Kitts-Nevis** (☎ 869-465-8571) and **Nevis Express** (☎ 869-469-9755 or 9756; www.nevisexpress.com). Flights cost US $25 each way.

Nevis Express also offers day trips to neighboring islands. On Wednesdays and Saturdays they do runs to St. Barts (US $100) and Sint Maarten (US $80). A unique offering is the flightseeing trip to the volcano on Montserrat for US $100; the flight is subject to weather conditions.

Nature Tours

Nevis is a hiker's dream. Walks of all difficulty levels are available both on a guided or a self-guided basis.

A great resource for hikers in search of Caribbean trails is ***The Caribbean: A Walking & Hiking Guide***, written by Leonard Adkins and available from Hunter Publishing (www.hunterpublishing. com).

> ⊚ **NOTE**
>
> Each of these trails receives only minimal maintenance, so hikers need to pack out all debris to minimize habitat destruction.

If you will be hiking without a guide, advise your concierge or someone else at your hotel of your proposed route. They can tell you of any potential problems along the routes (such as wash-outs after heavy rains). Be sure to bring along plenty of water on any of these treks; you won't be passing concession facilities along the way. Socks and closed shoes are advised for all hikes.

Some of Nevis' most popular treks include the following:

⊚ **The Source**. This excursion takes about four hours (round trip) from the Golden Rock Hotel, 10 miles southwest of airport. Maps are available at the hotel and lead hikers up to "the source" of Nevis' fresh water. The trail winds past a deep ravine, up through the rain forest, and to a waterfall. Along the way, hikers have good views of St. Kitts but should be prepared to get muddy on what's often a slippery trail. The hike ends at a 120-foot ladder to the water source. Bathing in this area is forbidden and is punishable by fine because this is the island's water supply.

◎ **Golden Rock Nature Walk**. The closest thing to a botanical garden on Nevis, this is a must-see for nature lovers. Head to the Golden Rock Hotel (see above) and pick up a map (50¢) for a self-guided walk. The hike is easy but wear good walking shoes. Allow about half an hour.

◎ **Nevis Peak.** The most strenuous hike on the island. The peak can be reached by two trails: the **Hamilton Trail** or the **Zetlands Trail** (more difficult, although shorter). Either route takes about five hours and runs through a variety of different ecosystems, starting at a dry evergreen forest and working up to an elfin woodland.

Rain jackets often come in handy on the Zetlands Trail hike (it is, after all, a rain forest).

◎ **Round Hill or Telegraph Hill**. From Mount Nevis Hotel and Beach Club, 10 miles north of the airport (see map), hikers can take off to the summit for views of Charlestown, Newcastle Airport, and nearby St. Kitts. The hike takes at least half an hour and is considered moderately strenuous.

◎ **Saddle Hill**. Ruins of an old British fortress are found at this volcanic peak on the southern end of the island. From here, hikers have a view of both the Caribbean and Atlantic. Saddle Hill is south of the Montpelier Estate, 10 miles southwest of Charlestown (see map).

Guided Hikes

Guided hikes offer the opportunity to learn more about the areas in which you're hiking. These operators offer excursions that range from gentle walks to heart-pumping hikes.

Eco-Tours Nevis, ☎ (869) 469-2091, offers four walking tours.

◎ **Historic Charlestown**. This 1½-hour walk begins at the birthplace of Alexander Hamilton, now the **Museum of Nevis History**, and takes a look at this Victorian-era West Indian town. The tour is scheduled for Sunday afternoons at 3 pm; the cost is US $10 per person.

◎ **Eco-Ramble**. This 2½-hour hike covers the east coast of Nevis and travels to the 18th-century **New River** and

Coconut Walk Estates to learn more about the diverse ecology of Nevis, discover archaeological evidence of pre-Colombian Amerindian settlers, and explore the remains of the last working sugar factory on Nevis. The hike is available Monday and Fridays at 9:30 am and Wednesdays at 3 pm; the cost is US $20 per person.

🌀 **The Sugar Trail Hike**. This walk looks at **Montravers House**, an abandoned great house. The 2½-hour trip is an easy hike into the tropical forest-covered slopes of **Nevis Peak**. The walk is available Tuesday and Saturday at 10 am; the cost is US $20 per person.

🌀 **Tower Hill Hike**. Travels past freshwater ponds and the ruins of a sugar mill before beginning the climb up **Nevis Peak**. The journey takes about 2½ hours and costs US $20.

Top to Bottom's Jim Johnson, ☎ (869) 469-5371, provides visitors with an enthusiastic look at the island's birds and plants. Call for prices. Some hikes offered by this operator include:

🌀 **Green Ghaut Hike**. This vine-filled valley is verdant with flowers, ferns, and philodendrons, which are identified for participants. This is a challenging hike.

- ◎ **Jessups Reservoir Hike**. Climb to the rain forest to learn more about the plants, birds, and insects on this moderately challenging hike.

- ◎ **Plantation Sunset Walk**. An easy walk, this route follows footpaths through an old estate to learn more about the island's botany as well as its history. Travelers see ruins, the oldest pond on Nevis, and wild donkeys.

- ◎ **Starlight and Storytime**. This nighttime excursion allows hikers to view the stars in Nevis' clear skies and also listen to the island's night sounds. The evening ends with a beach campfire and the chance to roast coconuts and marshmallows.

Heb's Nature Tours, ☎ (869) 469-2501, offers a half-hour hike to **Herbert's Heights Nature Preserve**. A gentle, sloping hillside, at 1200 feet above sea level, the preserve has the same panorama of vistas as Nevis Peak, without the steep climb. This mountainside reserve is located in the **Rawlins** area of the island and is especially notable for its rich flora and fauna. Plants include mango, mammee apple, and cocoa. At a bamboo orientation center, guides lead visitors up a trail to the edge of the rain forest. A self-guided interpretive trail is also available with a lookout tower and covered picnic area equipped with a telescope to view neighboring islands.

Sunrise Tours, ☎ (869) 469-2758, lists several guided hikes. Call for prices.

- ◎ **Nevis Peak**. A challenging hike, this morning excursion to the top of the peak offers views of Montserrat, Saba, St. Kitts and Antigua.

- ◎ **Nevis Village Walk**. This is a leisurely stroll through **Charlestown** for a look at traditional homes and stores.

- ◎ **Saddle Hill (Nelson's Lookout) Hike**. The scenic hike follows trails that include views of St. Kitts, Redonda, Montserrat and Antigua. Guides point out medicinal plants along the way, and you may glimpse a vervet monkey.

- ◎ **Source Trail Hike**. This guided walk up to the source of Nevis' fresh water takes about three hours.

Island Sightseeing

Nevis' greatest asset is its natural beauty, a curtain of green lushness that envelops Mount Nevis as it rises from the sea. Covered with a blanket of tall coconut palms, the hillsides invite slow drives and long walks. For most travelers, the greatest attractions to Nevis are its eco-tourism activities, leisurely resort pace, and golden beaches. Most travelers spend a day, however, exploring some of the island's other charming sights.

Charlestown

It's worth a walking tour of Charlestown to enjoy its Caribbean architecture and historic homes. Once called "a sink of debauchery," today Charlestown is a sleepy little town that has proven to be a genuine survivor. Over the past 300 years, this city has weathered fires, earthquakes, hurricanes and warfare but has maintained the charming appeal still seen in its Victorian-era West Indian buildings. Because many of the early stone structures were destroyed by earthquakes in the 1800s, after that time residents began the practice of building a first floor made of stone and an upper floor made of wood. Guided tours of this city are available from **Eco-Tours Nevis**, ☎ (869) 469-2091, and **Sunrise Tours**, ☎ (869) 469-2758.

BUREAU OF TOURISM
across from Dr. D.R. Walwyn Plaza, Charlestown

Stop by the Bureau of Tourism for brochures, maps, and information on the island. The office is open Monday and Tuesday, 8 am to 4:30 pm; Wednesday through Friday, 8 am to 4 pm; Saturday, 10 am to 1 pm; and Sundays, whenever a cruise ship is in port.

MARKET PLACE

On Tuesday, Thursday and Saturday mornings, stop by the market place for a real slice of Caribbean life. Fresh fruit, spices and vegetables.

BATHS HOTEL AND SPRING HOUSE
Main Street, Charlestown; no phone

Nevis island tours usually include a stop at the ruins of the Bath Hotel, built in 1778 for wealthy Nevisians to bask in 108° waters (until recently, modest facilities were open for visitors to "take the waters"). When it was built, the hotel was considered the most ambitious structure ever built in the West Indies. The waters, said to contain sulphur, ammonium, and magnesium, were sought by those looking for relief from arthritis and rheumatism. Five tile-lined booths offered a chance for a soak in the curative hot waters; visitors just climbed down the steps into the booth. Currently the baths are not open for soaks, however.

MUSEUM OF NEVIS HISTORY
Main Street, Charlestown
☎ (869) 469-5786

This small museum includes exhibits on indigenous people, Nevis' first residents approximately 4,000 years ago. Other displays cover the island's political history, slavery, home crafts, churches, and more. The museum is housed in the home that was the birthplace of Alexander Hamilton, first Secretary of the US Treasury. Exhibits recall the life of this famous Nevis resident. The museum is open Monday through Saturday. If you visit one of Nevis' museums, admission to the second (see Horatio Nelson Museum, below) is half price.

CRUISE SHIP TERMINAL
Charlestown

Nevis' cruise terminal marks some of the newest construction on the island. The waterfront here sports a new face with gazebos, benches, and, soon, shopping.

HANDICRAFT COOPERATIVE
Main Street, Charlestown
☎ (869) 469-1746

Located near the Bureau of Tourism, this little shop is a must for arts and crafts shoppers and anyone looking to bring back a Nevisian souvenir. Look for wood carvings, small artwork, and even Nevisian honey here.

JEWISH CEMETERY
Government Road, Charlestown

Once a large population of Sephardic Jews called Nevis home (making up as much as 25% of the island's population), many coming to the island from Brazil. In the 17th century, Nevis was home to both a synagogue and a Jewish cemetery, with tombstones dating back to 1658. The cemetery is reached along a stone-walled path that's locally known as the "Jews' Walk" and "Jews' Alley." Nineteen tombstones mark gravesites at this cemetery.

JEWISH SYNAGOGUE
Government Road, Charlestown

The ruins of a Jewish synagogue dating back to 1688 are found just off the roadside in Charlestown. The site has been the location of several archaeological digs. Records in Amsterdam trace the building back to 1688, which would make it older than the Caribbean's official first synagogue in Curaçao that dates back to 1732.

Out-of-Town Sights

NELSON MUSEUM
next to Governor's House, Belle Vue
☎ (869) 469-0408

The name Horatio Nelson is mentioned throughout the Caribbean (see page 200 for more on this man) as a naval hero. The Englishman came to the region as an enforcer of England's Navigation Acts and was assigned to English Harbour, Antigua. In 1785, he came to Nevis. Two years later, the seaman married Nevisian widow Fanny Nisbet at a ceremony at Montpelier estate on March 11, 1787. Fanny Nisbet was given away by the future King of England, Prince William Henry (William IV).

Nelson went on to become England's greatest naval hero. Even today "the Nelson Touch" is a phrase used to describe the loyalty of men to their leader. The Admiral died at the battle of Trafalgar at the age of 47. Today his life is remembered at the Nelson Museum, the largest collection of Nelson memorabilia in the Western hemisphere. Paintings, china, figurines, and remembrances of the naval leader are found here, along with displays on Nevisian history. The finest museum in St. Kitts and Nevis, it is well worth a visit. The museum is run by the Nevis Historical and Conservation Society. Hours are Monday to Friday,

9 am to 4 pm and Saturday, 10 am to 1 pm. Admission is US $2 for adults, $1 for children.

SADDLE HILL AND NELSON'S LOOKOUT

South of the Montpelier Estate, 25 minutes west of airport. See the island map for driving route, which is difficult to give as there are no street names here!

Located at 1,850 feet, this great stone fortress built around 1740 was once Horatio Nelson's lookout for enemy ships. Visitors have a good view of Redonda, Montserrat, St. Kitts and Saba from these heights.

ST. JAMES ANGLICAN CHURCH
outskirts of Brick Kiln Village, on the northeast side of the island (take Main Road)

Only two other churches in the Caribbean contain statuary of a black Jesus: one in Haiti and another in Trinidad. This historic church, still used by local residents for weekly services, is also notable for another unique feature. The church is the burial place of former parishioners, with gravestones dating back to the late 1600s and early 1700s, set into the flooring.

EDEN BROWN ESTATE
On the main road just south of Mannings

These ruins, formerly an estate of a wealthy planter, were the site of a true tragedy. The legend goes that on the eve of his wedding a bridegroom planter and his best man got into a duel and both men were killed. The bride-to-be went mad and is said to haunt the ruins today. The site

Ready for a little ghost story? Time to make a stop at the Eden Brown Estate.

is grown over and is little more than a few stone walls, but for those with an active imagination it's an interesting stop.

$ Shop Till You Drop

Stamp collectors will be familiar with Nevis because its stamps are sought-after items. Stop by the **Philatelic Bureau** in Charlestown for the best selection. It's located in the main post office on Main Street; call for hours, ☎ (869) 469-0617.

Fashion Boutiques

ISLAND HOPPER
TDC Plaza, Charlestown
☎ (869) 469-0893

Island Hopper has been in business for over 20 years and sells many local fashions.

Local Crafts, Gifts & Souvenirs

NEVIS POTTERY
Main Road, Newcastle; no phone

One of the best stops in Newcastle, where artisans craft the local clay into various vessels. The pots are finished over a fire of coconut shells behind the shop. It is open Monday through Friday and is located near the Newcastle Airport.

Nevis

ISLAND HOPPER
TDC Plaza, Charlestown
☎ (869) 469-0893

One of the most popular shops in town. A great place to find gifts for your friends back home, or a memento of your vacation!

NEVIS HANDICRAFT CO-OP
Main Street, Charlestown
☎ (869) 469-1746

This is the perfect place to find something unique to bring back to your friends and family. Crafts, hot sauces, and other local foods will give your loved ones a taste of what your vacation was like.

Nevis After Dark

Nightlife in Nevis is a pretty limited topic for discussion. Most travelers spend the evening enjoying a fine meal, followed by some quiet stargazing.

There is some entertainment, mostly during high season. Check with the **Golden Rock Plantation Inn** (☎ 869-469-3346) and the **Oualie Beach Hotel** (☎ 869-469-9735) for their scheduled entertainment. Also try the **Four Seasons Resort Nevis** (☎ 869-469-1111), which often has something going on.

Nevis A-Z

Banks

Bank of Nevis Ltd.
Main Street, Charlestown
☎ (869) 469-5564

Nevis Co-op Banking Co. Ltd.
Chapel Street
☎ (869) 469-5277

Dentists

Dr. Victor Hill
Government Road, Charlestown
☎ (869) 469-1361

Emergency Phone Numbers

Ambulance . . . . ☎ 911
Fire . . . . ☎ 333
Police . . . . ☎ 911
Police Information Line . . . . ☎ 707

Grocery Stores

Thompson Owen
Gingerland
☎ (869) 469-3663

Hospital

Alexandria Hospital
☎ (869) 469-5521

Optical Services

Caribbean Optical Eye Clinic
GMBC Building, Government Road, Charlestown
☎ (869) 469-0406

Pharmacies

Evelyn's Drug Store
Main Street, Charlestown
☎ (869) 469-5278

Olsen Pharmacy LTD
North Memorial Square Road, Charlestown
☎ (869) 469-0212

Photo Labs

Pemberton's Photo & Video Services
Main Street, Charlestown
☎ (869) 469-5879

Places of Worship

New Testament Church Of God
Fountain Village
☎ (869) 469-9542

Shiloh Baptist Church
Ramsbury Site, Charlestown
☎ (869) 469-5007

Zion Gospel Chapel
Aion Hill, Gingerland
☎ (869) 469-3014

Post Office

Charlestown, ☎ (869) 469-5221

Room Tax

There's 7% room tax, with a 10% service charge added to your bill.

Telephone Service

International Directory Inquiries. . ☎ 412
Local Directory Inquires . . . . ☎ 411

Website

www.stkitts-nevis.com

Appendix

Internet Sites

www.adventureantigua.com
Adventure Antigua, offering tours on Antigua.

www.allegroresorts.com
Allegro Resorts, Antigua.

www.antiguavillas.com
Antigua Villas

www.westindian.com/backhome
News from the West Indies.

www.candw.kn
Cable and Wireless, St. Kitts and Nevis directory.

www.candoo.com/carib
Site of Carib Aviation, offering inter-island flights.

http://caribbeanhighlights.com/Helicopter/default.htm
Caribbean Helicopters site. Based in Antigua, this company offers charter flights to other islands too.

www.caribbeans.com
Caribbean Information Office. An e-travel agent offering flights, hotels and useful links.

www.caribtourism.com
Caribbean Tourism Organization. Good general

information and referrals to Caribbean travel agents.

www.caribrepvillas.com
Caribrep, Villa Rentals in Antigua.

www.caribseek.com
Caribseek, the Caribbean search engine.

www.caribsurf.com
Caribbean information, calendar of events, festivals, etc.

www.caribvillas.com
Villas on all islands.

www.curtainbluff.com
Curtain Bluff Hotel, Antigua.

www.ecoseatours.com
Eco Sea Tours, with bases in Antigua & Barbuda.

www.fourseasons.com
Four Seasons, Nevis.

www.galleonbeach.com
Galleon Beach Club, Antigua.

www.goldenlemon.com
Golden Lemon Inn and Villas, St. Kitts.

www.golden-rock.com
Golden Rock Estate, Nevis.

www.hawksbill.com
Hawksbill Resort, Antigua.

www.hermitagenevis.com
Hermitage Plantation Inn, Nevis.

http://caribbeansupersite.com
Island Connoisseur. All kinds of island information.

www.montpeliernevis.com
Montpelier Plantation Inn, Nevis.

www.nrca.org
Natural Resources Conservation Authority

www.nevisexpress.com
Nevis Express offers airline service to several islands.

www.nevis1.com
Nevis, West Indies, offering information and local links.

www.nisbetplantation.com
Nisbet Plantation Beach Club, Nevis.

www.occanterraceinn.net
Ocean Terrace Inn, St. Kitts.

www.antigua-barbuda.org
The official Antigua and Barbuda Website.

www.stkitts-nevis.com
The official St. Kitts and Nevis Website.

www.ottleys.com
Ottley's Plantation Inn, Nevis.

www.oualie.com
Oualie Beach Hotel, Nevis.

www.rawlinsplantation.com
Rawlins Plantation, St. Kitts.

www.royalpalmvillas-nevis.com
Royal Palm Villas, Villas.

www.sandals.com
Sandals Antigua Resort and Spa, Antigua.

www.travelfacts.com/tfacts/htm/stk/stkdest.htm
St. Kitts and Nevis destination page.

www.stkittsnevis.net
St. Kitts and Nevis Government Site

www.sknlabourparty.org
St. Kitts and Nevis Labour Party

www.sunsail.com
Sunsail Club. Sailing school in Colonna, Antigua, complete with accommodations.

www.tropicalresort.com
Tropical Resort, villa rentals on all islands.

Bibliography

Didcott, Charles and Christine. *St. Barth: French West Indies*. W.W. Norton & Co., 1997.

Doyle, Chris. *Cruising Guide to the Leeward Islands, 2000-2001.* Cruising Guide Publications, 2000.

Eiman, William J. (ed.). *Cruising Guide St. Maarten/St. Martin Area to Antigua and Barbuda.* Wescott Cove Publishing Co., 1992.

Gravette, Andy G. *French Antilles.* Hippocrene Books, Inc., 1991.

Henderson, James. *The Northeastern Caribbean: The Leeward Islands* (Cadogan Island Studies). Cadogan Books, 1994.

Hubbard, Vince. *Swords Ships and Sugar : A History of Nevis to 1900.* Premiere Editions Intl., 1993.

Huber, Joyce and Jon. *Best Dives of the Caribbean, 2nd Ed.* Hunter Publishing, 1999.

Luntta, Karl and Gina Wilson Birtcil (eds.) *Caribbean Handbook: The Virgin, Leeward, and Windward Islands.* Moon Publications, 1995.

Permenter, Paris and John Bigley. *Adventure Guide to Antigua, Barbuda, Nevis, St. Barts, St. Kitts & St. Martin, 2nd Ed.* Hunter Publishing, 2001.

Philpott, Don. *Antigua & Barbuda Landmark Visitors Guide.* Hunter Publishing, 2000.

Ryan, Colleen and Brian Savage. *The Complete Diving Guide: The Caribbean, Volume 2.* Complete Dive Publications, 1999.

Schnabel, Jerry and Susan L. Swygert. *Diving and Snorkeling Guide to St. Maarten, Saba, and St. Eustatius.* Pisces Books, 1994.

Stone, Robert. *Day Hikes on St. Martin* (The Day Hikes Series). ICS Books, 1996.

Street, Donald M., Jr. *Street's Cruising Guide to the Eastern Caribbean: Anguilla to Dominica* (Street's Cruising Guide). W.W. Norton & Co., 1993.

Index